Quilted Postcards – The Art Edition

'Little Quilts Of Creativity'

By Sarah Sparkes

www.tortoisecrafts.co.uk

Postcard design, text and artwork © 2023 Sarah Sparkes

Photography © 2023 Tony Sparkes

Editing Tony Sparkes

Proof Reading Laura Sparkes

Published by Tortoise Crafts Publishing
All enquiries to: editor@tortoisecraftspublishing.co.uk

First Edition

First published 2023

ISBN: 978-1-8380342-3-8

Dedication

To my husband, Tony, who made this possible.

To our daughter, Laura, for all the proof reading.

To my best friend, Rachel, for all the
encouragement over the years.

To Eileen, for reading my many drafts.

And to my Mother-in -law & Tony's Mum,
Pat Sparkes, a true crafter to the end, you will be
sadly missed.

Thank you.

Sarah

Contents

Introduction

This is the fourth book in the Quilted Postcard series. It seemed the natural progression after writing the first three to write this one on the 'Art' Quilted Postcards that I create.

I have been creating the 'Art' postcards for a number of years, they started off with me trying to create, in fabric, places we had been and taken photos of. The first ones were of our holiday in Cornwall way back in 2009. Over the years I learnt the limitations of the 6" x 4" size and what I felt worked and didn't and eventually my style of Art Quilted Postcards emerged.

The Art Postcards are inspired by the English landscapes, gates, doors, crumbling structures, dry stone walls, planters and the gardens of the National Trust and the ironwork of the Victorian era. On our holidays and days out we take a huge amount of photos, we have thousands and thousands of them!!! These photos are the basis and inspiration of many of my postcards. I no longer try to copy the photos but I use them to inspire and use elements of them. Sometimes I use a number of photos, a pot here, a watering can from another and an arch from another.

The embroidered flowers aren't accurate representations. They are my 'take' on the flowers, using a few basic stitches to give the feel of plants and flowers.

I will often make up two or three using the same basic design but each one will be different. The embroidered flowers will be different shapes and colours, no two are the same! They are unique.

With this book I want to inspire you to create similar Quilted Postcards, by showing you how I create mine, giving you the inspiration and skills to create your own pieces of 'Art' Quilted Postcards.

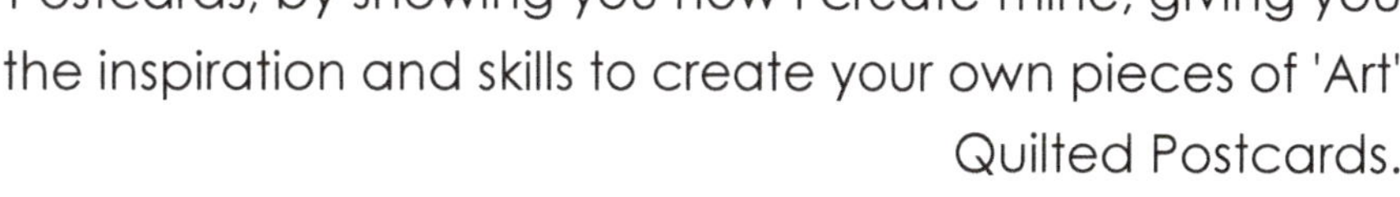

What is a Quilted Postcard?

A Quilted Postcard is a 6" x 4" piece of fabric art made using three layers – front, wadding and back. The size makes it a postcard and the three layers make it a quilt. They use the skills of machine patchwork and quilting, but are embellished with drawing and hand embroidery, this combination makes them 'Little Quilts of Creativity'. They are perfect as gifts to send to those special someone's, either on their own or mounted onto a card. They can also be framed and put on the wall as Art.

How to use this book

This book follows along similar lines to our previous three but has a lot more photos of the stages and explanations, mostly of the embroidery. The embroidery section shows the most commonly used plants and flowers that I embroider on the postcards. Please read this and then the first Postcard. The Garden Gate has detailed instructions needed to make a Quilted Postcard, explaining how I create them, and I would recommend even if you have made postcards before to read through this one – these Art Quilted Postcards, although made in a similar way to all the others I make have a few quirks and there are different hints and tips to help creating them. For all the other postcards I have only included specifics for that postcard.

Throughout this book you will find  "*Patch*", my logo. She marks where I give my personal hints and tips to help you make the Postcards.

Happy Creating!

Sarah

Basic Supplies

These are the basic things that I use in making Quilted Postcards. It is only a suggested list, I could write a huge great big list of things, especially colours of threads but I believe that it is better for you to use what you find works and is best for you.

Fabrics

As I am a Patchwork Quilter and these Quilted Postcards are an offshoot from making quilts, I have always used 100% cotton designed for patchwork, it comes in a huge range of colours and shades. I keep the fabric I use for these Art Quilted Postcards in a separate stash from my quilt fabrics, as it is easier to find what I want – I have collected a range of greens, sky blues and stone/gravel colours in plains, mottles and small tonal prints. Many I just buy a Fat Quarter others that I know I will use a lot I buy in full metres, whenever I see something I think will work I buy it!!! For the back of the postcard I use a white cotton fabric. I buy a better quality bleached calico (USA muslin) for this.

Threads

I use a big range of threads on my Sewing Machine. I have lots of thread in my workroom and I use whichever works best with the current project, from standard sewing cotton, sew-all to rayons for embroidery and machine quilting threads, from plains to variegated threads. I have so many shades of green but the most used is a very dark green (Gutermann Sew All col 472). In my bobbin I use a standard white cotton thread on all the projects.

Stranded Embroidery Cotton

I use DMC, and as I also do cross stitch and so does our daughter, we have boxes and boxes of threads. If you don't have any then I would recommend buying just those that you need. The variegated ones that DMC do are really good and I go through a lot of greens 92 & 94, plus I love 48, 52, 90, 105, 115 & 121 for flowers.

Wadding (Batting)

All the wadding that I use is leftovers/offcuts from my patchwork quilting. As I prefer to use 80/20 Cotton/Polyester wadding like Hobbs Heirloom, it is also used in the postcards and other bits. I would recommend a wadding that doesn't mind being pressed, so not a polyester one.

Iron On interfacing

I use Vlieseline H200 interfacing, as I find it firm enough to give the postcards and other bits the 'body' I want but not so thick that it makes it really tough on my hands for the hand embroidery. But use the product that you prefer, as long as it is white and iron-on. Follow the manufacturers instructions for pressing the interfacing onto the fabric.

Sewing Machine

Although a sewing machine isn't essential for creating Quilted Postcards it does make them quicker and easier to do, especially finishing the edges. Every sewing machine is different, you know your machine best and the stitches it does and the best threads for it. I use mostly three stitches to create the Postcards, straight, zig zag and blanket (applique) stitch, but use what you prefer. I also prefer to use my walking foot (Even feed foot), I do all my quilting on quilts with it.

I would suggest that you have a bit of a 'play' with the settings on your machine, till you find the stitches and stitch width and lengths that you are happy with – remember to make a note of the settings. Please remember that I make suggestions on threads and stitches but they are my preferences, you will have your own.

I guess I should tell you that I use Bernina sewing machines. The one I use mostly is an Aurora 440qe. I also have two others an Activa 135 for taking out to classes and my original 1130 that I bought a long time ago!!

Fabric Marking Pens & Pencils

I use a normal pencil for a lot of the marking. Please check that whichever pencil you use for drawing on the fusible web, doesn't come off onto the iron, as it is really annoying to find that you have ruined a piece of fabric because the pencil has come off on to it! Especially a pale colour.

For marking on details to be embroidered I use Clover Air erasable pen, or Clover Chalk pencils. These come in a pack of four colours – white, yellow, blue & pink with a sharpener. I can get them nice and sharp pointed to draw fine lines.

For drawing on details like dry stone walls and also for writing on the back of the postcards I use a Sukura Pigma Micron Archival Ink Black. I have them in a number of different thicknesses but the one I use most is a No.3.

Scissors

My preferred scissors are my Fiskars embroidery and Fiskars General purpose 16.5cm ones. These get used for everything!!! I know scissors should only be used for fabric, but I use these for fabric, fusible web and paper. I find them a nice size and weight.

Rotary Cutter, Mat & Rulers

If you have them then use them, if you haven't then scissors are as good. I would recommend a good straight solid ruler for measuring and marking, it doesn't have to be a big one. I find the 1" x 14" one is really good for this as is a 6½" square.

Iron & Ironing Mat

Whatever you usually use. I have a separate iron and ironing mat that I use only for patchwork because, however careful I am accidents will happen, and fusible web and interfacing will get stuck to the iron or ironing mat.

Please remember to clean the sole plate on your iron regularly. The cover on my ironing mat is removable and made from brushed cotton cot sheets (they were Laura's!!!). I put them in the wash every couple of weeks.

Fusible Web

Use your favourite one – mine is Vlieseline Bondaweb, a paper backed thin layer of glue. I buy a whole box as I go through so much of it. I wouldn't necessarily recommend buying this amount, unless you going to make a lot of stuff. I have found it is best to keep it rolled and, in a box, away from heat and sunlight.

Odif 505 Temporary Adhesive spray

This is optional but I find it useful.

Hand Sewing Needles, Thimble & Pins

Whatever you find best and prefer.

Please note I am not sponsored by any company or manufacturer. All the products I have mentioned are ones that I have, over the years, used and preferred on a personal basis.

Embroidery Stitches

I mainly use three proper embroidery stitches for the details. I do also use random different length stitches for things like grass or to add texture. I have given basic instructions for Split Stitch, French knot and Lazy Daisy Stitch but like everything else in this book, it is only what I use, please use whatever stitches you want to.

French Knot

1) Bring the threaded needle up where you want the French knot to be.

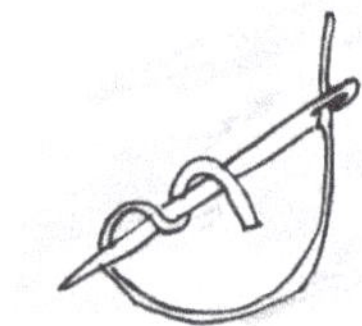

2) Hold the needle horizontal to the fabric and wrap the thread round the needle, two or three times, holding the thread taut.

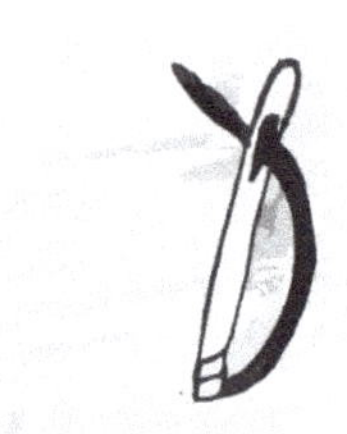

3) Insert the needle through the fabric, right next to where it came out, keeping the thread taut and pull the needle through the fabric to form the knot.

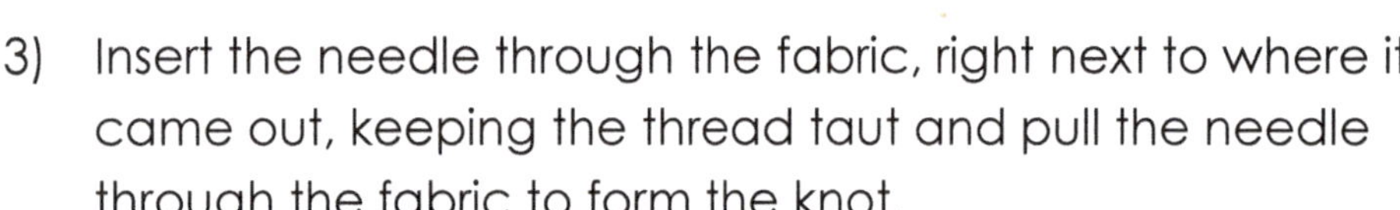

I have seen different ways to stitch a French Knot but I have shown the way I use. I will admit that French Knots take practice to get right!!

The number of times I wrap the thread round the needle depends on the look I am trying to get, twice round creates a smaller knot, three times a bigger one. By holding the thread taut as I pull the needle through gives a tight knot, if you want a baggier knot don't hold it taut. And finally I don't go back down the hole the thread comes out, as it is more likely for the knot to disappear and slip to the back!!! I insert the needle just next to it.

Split Stitch

1) Bring the threaded needle up to the front of the fabric at the start of the line to be stitched and create one basic stitch.

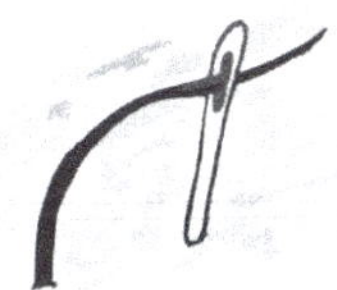

2) Then bring the needle back through to the front of the fabric a third of the way down the first stitch, 'splitting' the thread.

3) Take the needle to the back of the fabric to finish the stitch. Continue creating stitches in this way.

I prefer the look of this stitch rather than the more common Back Stitch. The other stitch that is similar in look to Split Stitch is Stem Stitch

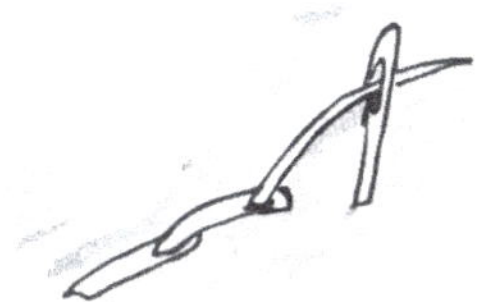

By changing the length of your stitch you can create a smooth line, so going round curves or circles I will use smaller stitches than on a straight line.

Lazy Daisy Stitch (And Chain Stitch)

1) Bring the threaded needle up where you want the stitch to start. Take it back down right next to it, but don't pull the eye through.

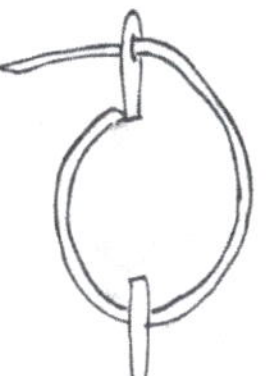

2) Bring the needle back up where you want the stitch to finish making sure the thread is sandwiched between the point of the needle and the fabric.

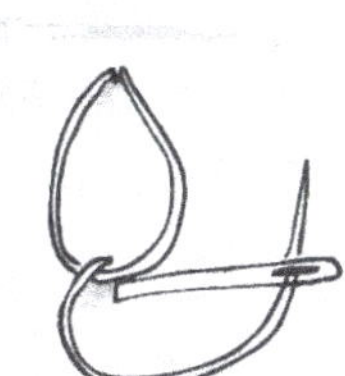

3) Pull the thread to form a loop.

4) Bring the needle down the other side of the thread, creating a small holding stitch.

Lazy Daisy Stitch is a single unit of Chain Stitch and is really good for flower petals.

Plant & Flower Stitches

I thought I would include some samples of the stages of how I stitch the plants & flowers that I use on the Quilted Postcards. I use the same basic stitches for all the plants, just how I put them together is different and change the look with different colours of thread.

Small Flowering Shrub

I start with the stem, stitching it in split stitch, followed by the leaves in individual Lazy Daisy Stitch and finally adding French Knot flowers. Its all stitched using two strands of embroidery cotton.

Small Ground Covering Plants

They start with lots of French Knots, the stems are added and then three French Knots are stitched at the top of each stem. I also stitch these plants without the stems, and have the green French Knots with the a layer of coloured ones on top.

Small Large Leaf Plants Like A Hosta

The large Lazy Daisy Stitches are stitched in a gentle curve, with the stems coming up from them, then I either stitch French Knots for the flowers or alternatively Lazy Daisy Stitches and then French Knots.

Small Flowering Plants Like Daffodils & Muscari

Stitch two large Lazy Daisy Stitches with a stem in the middle, then the flower can be either a cone of French Knots, three or four Lazy Daisy Stitches hanging down with French Knot on top, or a flower head of Lazy Daisy Stitches with a French Knot in the middle. Or any combination of the stitches.

Climbing Rose

The woody stems are stitched in stem or split stitch, often I will use two colours, like dark brown and dark green together. The leaves are individual Lazy Daisy Stitch, and I will use three or four shades of similar green thread for them. The rose flowers are lots of French Knots.

Flowering Shrub Rose

These are worked in the same way as the climbing roses but just smaller. The stems are stitched first, then the leaves of Lazy Daisy Stitch and the flowers are French Knots.

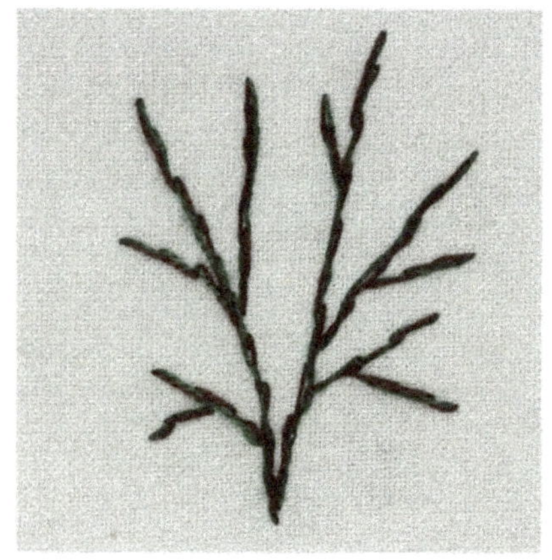

Flowering Plants Like Dahlias

The stems are stitched in a darker green using split stitch, with the leaves stitched next. I don't stitch leaves right at the end of the stems as the flowers are stitched on them, a circle of Lazy Daisy Stitch with a French knot in the middle. Often with the flowers I will stitch either two different colours, as in the sample – a variegated yellow and pink, or two different shades of the same colour to give more interest.

Flowering Plants

This type of flowering plant is just three stems with the leaves stitched on and then lots of French Knots along the stems for flowers and berries.

Tall Plants Like Verbena

These are tall background plants and are stitched in only one strand of thread for both the stems and the small French Knots for the flowers.

Cow Parsley Type Plants

The stem is stitched in two strands and then the spikes of the flowers are in a single strand of the same green. The Flowers are French Knots, for more depth, and a stronger look, I will use two strands of thread, for a more delicate look I will use just one strand. I mostly stitch the flowers in white but occasionally in green.

Tall Thistle Like Plants

I stitch the long stems with a few leaves in straight stitch and French Knots, I sometimes leave it like that or sometimes add more leaves down the stem with a single strand of thread.

Tall Plants Like Foxgloves, Lupins, Delphiniums & Hollyhocks

I start with stitching the long straight stem, from the bottom to the top and then I stitch three French Knots just down from the top, one on one side and two on the other side of the stem, the leaves start at the top as normal Lazy Daisy Stitch and as I go down, I do bigger ones with two bars to change the shape. I fill the leaves in with a few straight stitches. For the flowers, depending on the type I want I will do either French Knots, bigger ones at the bottom – three twists of thread round the needle and then at the very top just two or one twist. Or I will do Lazy Daisy Stitch to start with and then French Knots. For Hollyhock type flowers I will create a circular flowers.

Starter Postcard—Garden Door

Even if you don't want to make this postcard first, please, please read through the instructions, there are lots of hints and tips that I have put in, that aren't in the others in this book. Things that I have worked out over years of trial and error and constantly learning what works and doesn't!!

I have a love of doors and gates – garden doors, especially walled garden ones! Field gates, wrought iron gates, just gates in general. I don't know what it is about them, but they are a very big source of inspiration.

<table>
<tr><td>You will need to make this Postcard</td><td>3 pieces of white cotton fabric 4½" x 6½"
2 pieces of iron-on interfacing 4½" x 6½"
1 piece of wadding 4" x 6"
Fusible web
A selection of fabric
A selection of sewing threads
A selection of stranded embroidery thread
Pigma archival pen
Chalk pencil and ruler
Air erasable pen</td></tr>
</table>

1) Select your fabrics for the background of the postcard, brown for the door, stone colour for the wall, and a shingle colour for the path.

I have a bag just for making the arty postcards, lots of shades of greens, fabrics for walls, paths and sky. They are plains, mottles or small tone on tone patterned fabrics. For this postcard, I have chosen a plain brown for the door, a sandstone mottled for the walls and a dotty sand colour for the path.

2) Take the fusible web and trace the three pieces, door, wall and path onto it.

3) Cut the pieces out of the fusible web, with a small allowance all round.

4) Press the fusible web onto the wrong side of each of the chosen fabrics.

Please note that on the Template design I have marked the wall and path with seam allowance on the edges of the postcard. If you cut them to the size of the postcard, which is marked by the dotted line, then it is harder to get a good finish to the edge, they come out better if made bigger and trimmed down.

All my designs are hand drawn, they are the correct size and also the way round for just putting the fusible web on top and tracing, so you don't have to enlarge or mirror image. They are ready to be used!

5) Cut the pieces out on the marked line.

6) Take one piece of the white cotton and one of the pieces of interfacing, press the interfacing onto one side of the cotton fabric.

7) Place the stabilised white cotton onto your ironing mat with the interfacing down, peel the backing paper off the wall, door and path and position on the cotton.

8) When happy that the pieces are positioned correctly, press in place.

9) Draw a 4" x 6" rectangle onto the front of the fabric.

10) On the door, draw the details using a
chalk pencil and ruler. Use both the
main photo and the drawing diagram
as a guide.

11) Layer the wadding and white cotton
onto the back of the prepared front.

I used the 505 temporary spray
adhesive to hold the layers together. If
you are using this, remember to spray it
only on the cotton wadding and in a
small amount.

12) Using straight stitch and dark brown sewing thread, stitch the details on the door and round the edge, remember to pull the threads to the back and tie off and trim as you go.

13) Stitch along the bottom of the wall and round the door frame.

14) Stitch round the front of the postcard on the marked rectangle.

15) Using an air erasable pen, draw lines up from the bottom of the wall every ½" to mark the stone blocks of the wall. For the stones above the door, draw a line following the curve of the door ½" above and then draw in the blocks.

16) Using the Pigma archival pen, draw in the blocks.

I will always draw in lines or a grid in an air erasable pen or chalk before I actually draw the stones, bricks or tiles onto postcards as that way if I haven't got something right I can redraw it. Also it gives me lines to work from, without them I would have very wonky blocks or bricks!!!

When drawing the blocks, use the lines to get the sizes but the stone blocks aren't perfect rectangles, the corners are a little rounded and the lines aren't straight. The blocks are weathered.

17) On the door, still using the Pigma pen, draw on the handle and then lightly shade in along the bottom, up the hinges' side and a bit of the curve at the top.

18) Start to embroider the plants and flowers. Start with the rose/flowering plant up the left hand side. Using two strands of embroidery cotton, embroider the stem.

19) Embroider on the leaves.

20) Embroider on the flowers.

21) Embroider the stems of the flowering plant on the right hand side.

22) Embroider on the leaves.

23) Embroider on the flowers.

24) Embroider the plants on the path.

25) Take the final piece of white cotton fabric and press the interfacing onto the wrong side. Place this on the back of the embroidered front, with the fabric facing outwards. Pin in place.

26) Stitch round just inside the marked
rectangle using a zig zag stitch.

28) Zig-zag round the Postcard again with
a slightly closer and wider stitch.

27) If you are using a rotary cutter, ruler
and mat, place your Postcard on the
mat, place the ruler along the marked
line and cut off the excess fabric. Or
you can cut along the lines with
scissors.

29) Using a pair of scissors, trim off the
'fluffy' bits on the edges and also the
ends of the threads.

30) Stitch round the edge for the third
time.

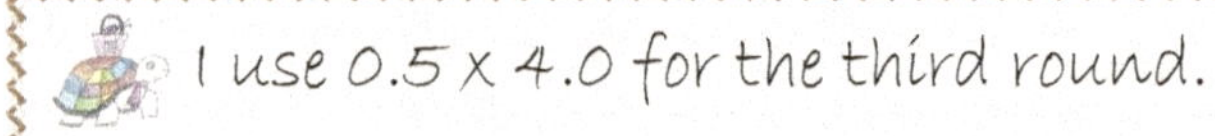

31) Again, using scissors, trim off the 'fluffy'
bits and the thread ends.

32) Stitch round the edge for the fourth
and final time.

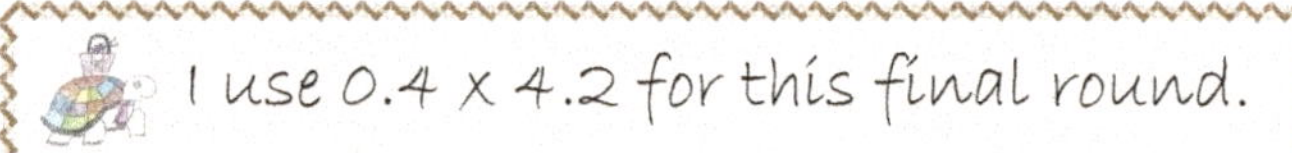

33) And go round again with the scissors
and trim off the 'fluffy' bits and the
thread ends.

34) Turn to the back of the Postcard and add any decoration that you wish.

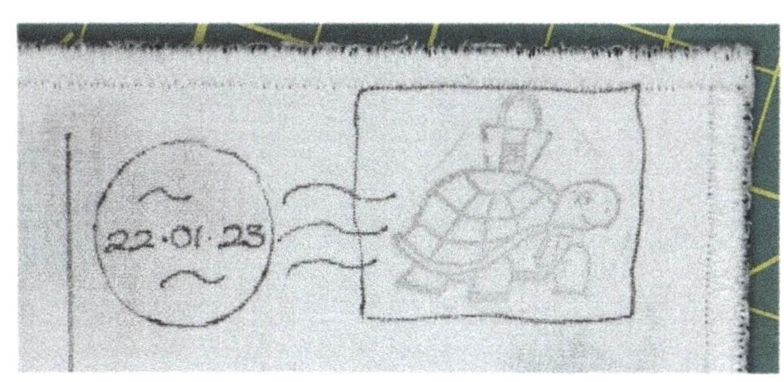

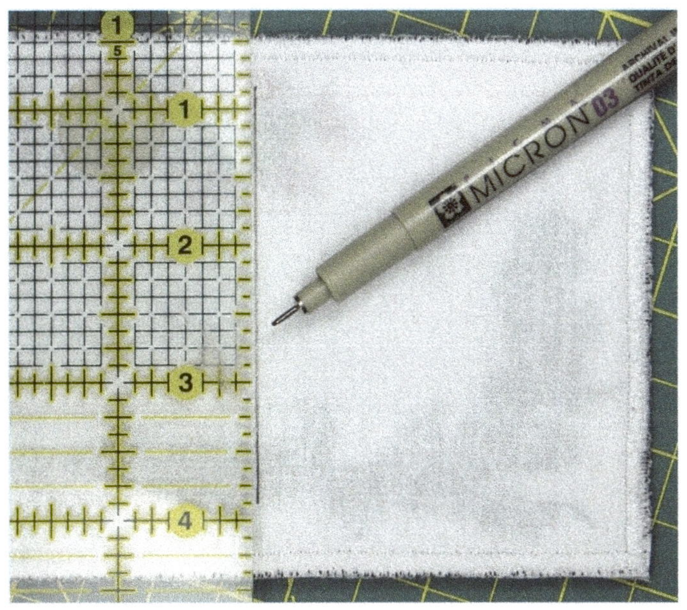

For all my Postcards I imitate a 'real' Postcard. The centre line is drawn using a ruler and Pigma Micron pen. I then stamp my 'makers' mark underneath the centre line. I create a postage stamp with a stamp of my logo. We had both rubber stamps specially created and I use a Versacraft black ink pad with them. Using the Pigma Micron pen, I draw a wobbly square round my logo for the postage stamp and then draw round an empty Gutermann 100m cotton reel to create the franking mark, the date is the date the Postcard was made.

A solid garden door
in a good solid red
brick wall with
summer blooms
growing round it.

I have so many
photos of
different garden
gates and
doors. This one
has big iron
hinges and
lighter
embroidered
plants. I was
trying to give it a
more Spring like
feel, with the
wisteria.

Oddly enough I have only read The
Secret Garden in the last year. This
door is inspired by the door being
overgrown and hidden, but with
my door you can still see parts of it,
unlike the one in the Secret
Garden book.

Detailed Template for Garden Door

Although there is a photo at the beginning, this sketch is the correct size of the finished Postcard. I always draw up a rough sketch when I have an idea for a new Postcard as it helps me visualise what the finished Postcard will look like. I have included a more 'polished' version of my sketch here to help you with placement of the stitches, drawn details etc.

Cutting Template for Garden Door

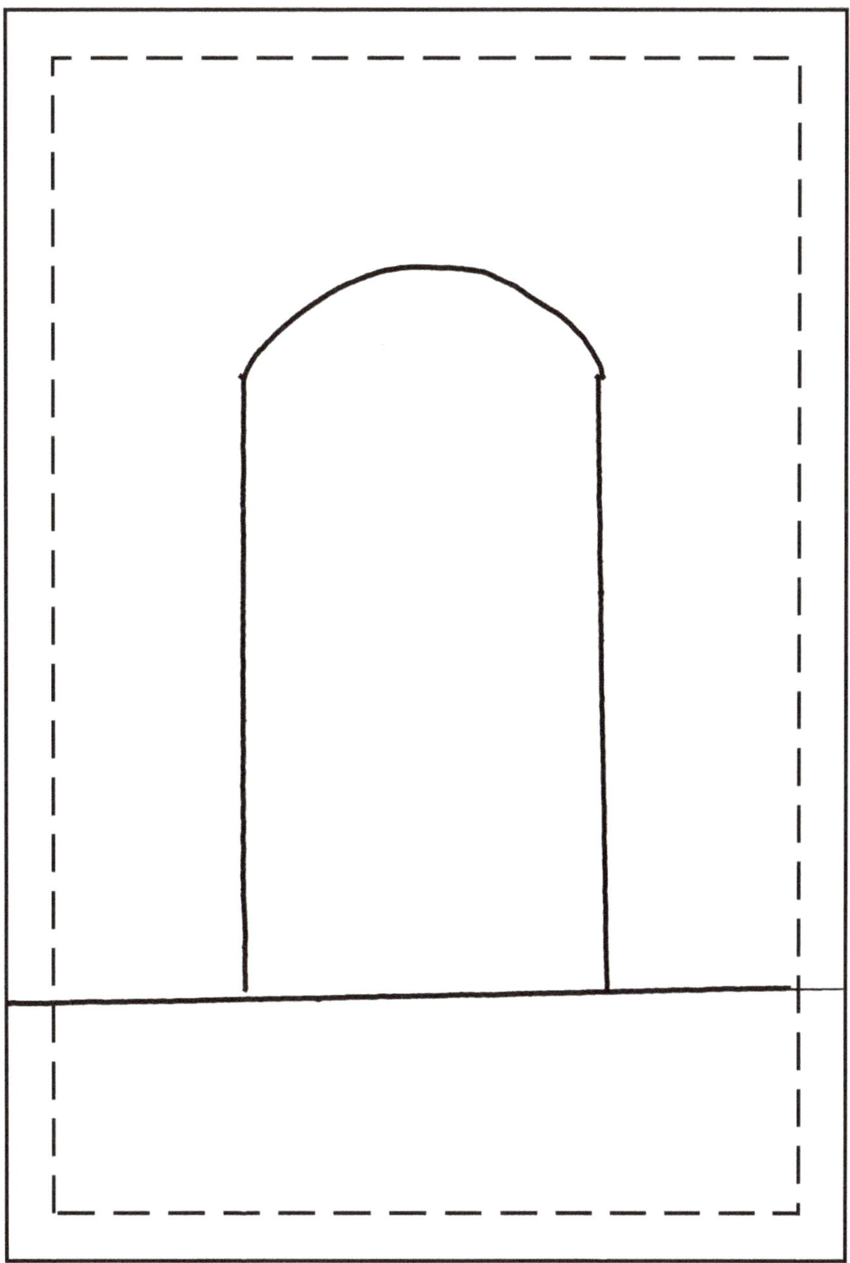

Just a reminder, all of my designs are hand drawn, they are the correct size and also the way round for just putting the fusible web on top and tracing, so you don't have to enlarge or mirror image. They are ready to be used!

All you need to do is to lay the fusible web, paper side up, onto this template and draw on the design.

Planters

I just have to look out of my kitchen window to get inspiration for planters, as most of my gardening is in containers!!! I constantly look for interesting planters when we are out from public parks, to National Trust estates there are always lots to find!!

You will need to make this Postcard

3 pieces of white cotton fabric 4½" x 6½"

2 pieces of iron-on interfacing 4½" x 6½"

1 piece of wadding 4" x 6"

Fusible Web

A selection of fabrics

A selection of sewing threads

A selection of stranded embroidery threads

Air erasable pen

1) Select the fabrics, for the wall, gravel and planters.

I have gone with warmer sandy shades for the gravel and wall and then greys for the big planter and the square one, then pink for the last one.

2) Take the fusible web and then trace all pieces onto it.

3) Cut the pieces out of the fusible web with a small allowance all round.

4) Press the fusible web onto the wrong side of the chosen fabrics.

5) Cut the pieces out on the marked line.

6) Take one piece of the white cotton fabric and press one piece of interfacing on the back.

7) Working on the cotton side, peel the backing paper off the wall and gravel first and place these down, then the big planter and finally the other two planters, press in place. Draw a 4" x 6" rectangle on the front.

8) Layer with the wadding and a piece of white cotton.

9) Stitch all the pieces and details and round the marked rectangle.

10) Stage one of the embroidery is the tree in the big planter.

12) Stage three of the embroidery is the plant in the pink planter.

11) Stage two of the embroidery is the leaves on the tree.

13) Stage four of the embroidery is the
    plants in the top of the pink planter.

14) The fifth and final stage of the
    embroidery is the plants in the dark
    grey square planter.

15) Press the interfacing to the back of the
    last piece of white cotton and then pin
    to the back of the postcard. Zig Zag
    round, cut off the excess fabric and
    then zig zag a number of times,
    making the stitch wider and tighter
    together, till you are happy with the
    finished edge.

This Urn was one of my earlier
planter inspired postcards and
again was inspired by the ones
in old gardens.

This old boot planter was
inspired by my Father-in-laws big
old work boots, battered and at
the end of life I could imagine
them as a really great planter.

Large stone troughs are a feature of many formal gardens, carved and then filled with lots of plants tumbling down over the edges.

A lot of the planter postcards that I create are inspired by the gardens of the National Trust, with the stone troughs and then lots of other pots around them, this one is a Spring themed postcard with dwarf narcissus, grape hyacinths, both the traditional blue/purple in the trough and also pink/white ones in the pot, and irises.

This large planter was inspired by a huge Victorian Urn in a public park, that stood on a big plinth in the middle of a flower bed, the Victorians did love their gardens, both private and public and they also went for large planters with formal seasonal planting.

Detailed Template for Planters

Cutting Template for Planters

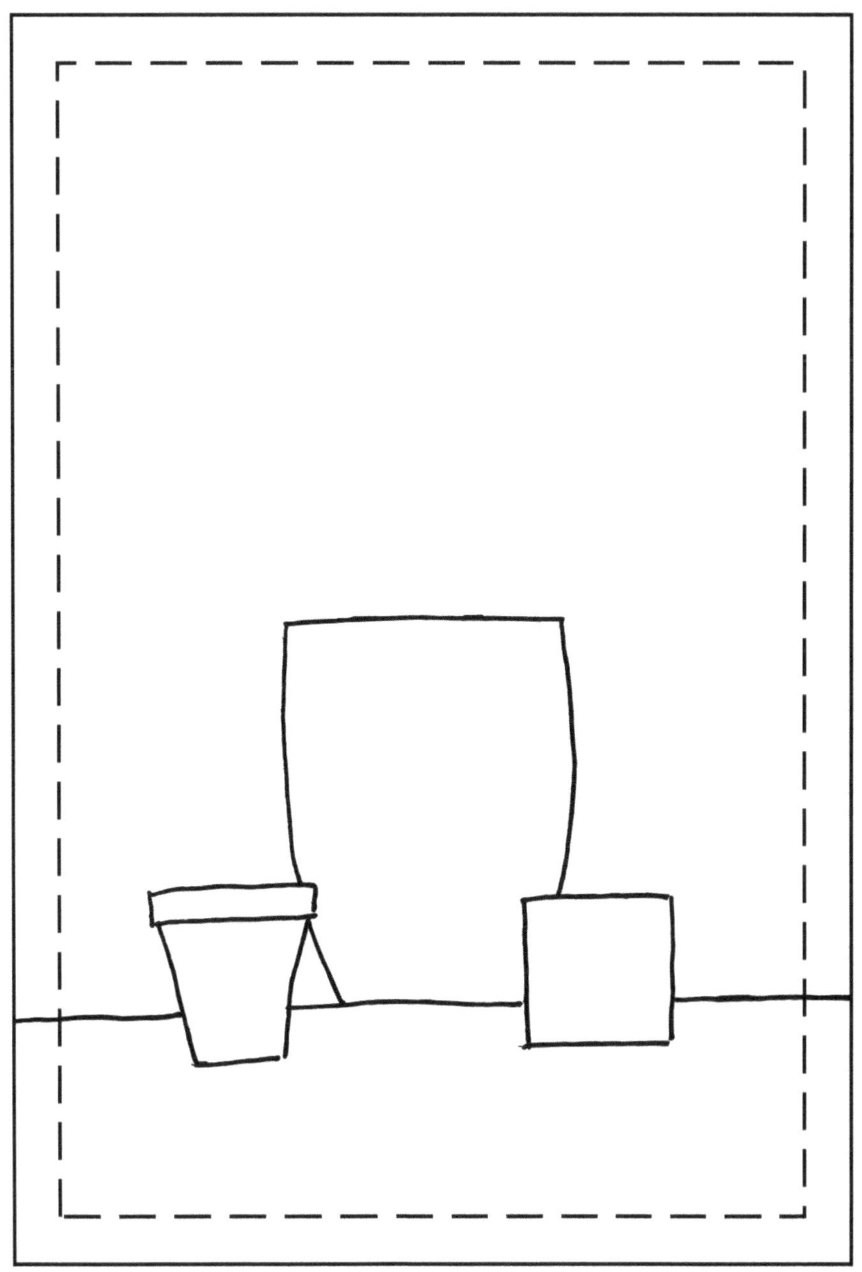

Crumbling Wall

Crumbling walls of ancient castles and garden follies, all feed into my imagination and this is where my ideas for these postcards come from. England is a land of old structures and legends..... King Arthur and Robin Hood, both of which I have always loved, the landscape is dotted with old interesting buildings.

You will need to make this Postcard

3 pieces of white cotton fabric 4½" x 6½"

2 pieces of iron-on interfacing 4½" x 6½"

1 piece of wadding 4" x 6"

Fusible Web

A selection of fabrics

A selection of sewing threads

A selection of stranded embroidery threads

Pigma Micron Archival Pen

Air erasable pen & Chalk pencils

1) Select the fabrics for the sky, fields and the wall.

I have used three shades of greens for the fields, two plain and a tone on tone one. For the wall I have used a mottled greyish toned fabric.

2) Take the fusible web and the trace all the pieces on.

3) Cut the pieces out of the fusible web with a small allowance all round.

4) Press the fusible web onto the wrong side of the chosen fabrics.

5) Cut the pieces out on the marked lines.

6) Take one piece of white cotton fabric and press one piece of the interfacing on the back.

7) Working on the cotton side, peel the backing paper off all the pieces. Start with sky and build up the fields and finally place the wall on top. Draw a 4" x 6" rectangle on the front.

8) Layer with the wadding and a piece of white cotton.

9) Stitch all the pieces and details and round the marked rectangle.

10) Draw the stone blocks on the wall.

12) Stage two of the embroidery is the moss, small plants growing in the cracks between the stone blocks on the wall.

11) Stage one of the embroidery is the shrubs and contour lines on the fields.

13) Stage three of the embroidery is the plants on the sill.

14) Stage four of the embroidery is the cow parsley at the centre bottom.

15) Stage five of the embroidery is the plant on the right-hand side.

16) Stage six of the embroidery is the foxgloves on the left hand side.

17) Stage seven of the embroidery is the grasses along the bottom.

18) Press the interfacing to the back of the last piece of white cotton and then pin to the back of the postcard. Zig Zag round, cut off the excess fabric and then zig zag a number of times, making the stitch wider and tighter together, till you are happy with the finished edge.

Inspirations

This postcard was inspired by a garden folly at a
National Trust estate, it looked like an old gothic
tower, it was built into a boundary wall between
the formal gardens and romantic wildness walk
beyond the gate.

The inspiration for this postcard is
an old castle wall that is falling
down and nature has softened
the edges with plants growing on
the top of the wall and in
between the stones.

The inspiration for this postcard is
Tintagel in Cornwall, the ruined
stone walls and arches, we took
lots of photos and over the years I
have used it as inspiration for a
number of postcards. This one
uses the arch but the background
and plants are imagination.

Detailed Template for Crumbling Wall

Cutting Template for Crumbling Wall

Just a reminder, all you need to do is to lay the fusible web, paper side up, onto this template and draw on the design. The template is already in mirror image.

Field Gate

Field gates – well actually all gates, fascinate me and I constantly come back to them as a source of inspiration for Quilted Postcards. This gate is a standard five bar one, that you see in many fields, more often or not they are made from metal nowadays but I love the old wooden ones.

You will need to make this Postcard

3 pieces of white cotton fabric 4½" x 6½"

2 pieces of iron-on interfacing 4½" x 6½"

1 piece of wadding 4" x 6"

Fusible web

A selection of fabrics

A selection of sewing threads

A selection of stranded embroidery threads

Pigma Archival Pen

Air erasable pen

1) Select the fabrics for the sky, back field, front field and the gate.

I have gone with tone on tone blue for the sky, sometimes a postcard needs a sky with a bit of a pattern, not a mottled. I went for a plain dark green for the back field to show off the gate, which is in a plain fabric and then a green fabric printed with grass for the front field.

2) Take the fusible web and trace all the design pieces onto it and cut out with a small seam allowance all round.

For the five bars of the fence and the gate, these are drawn and cut as long strips 1/8" wide by 6½" long as its less fiddly than having lots of small pieces.

3) Press the fusible web onto the wrong side of the chosen fabric.

4) Cut out the pieces on the marked lines.

5) Take one piece of the white cotton fabric and press one piece of interfacing on the back.

6) Working on the cotton side, peel the backing paper off the sky, back field and front field, put these in place first and press, then work on laying the strips for the five bars of the fence and gate across the width of the postcard. Place the posts across the bars and add the X bars on the gate. When happy with the placement of the fence and gate press in place. Draw a 4" x 6" rectangle on the front.

7) Layer with the wadding and a piece of white cotton fabric.

8) Machine applique all the pieces of the gate and fence.

9) Using a Micron Pen draw on the hinges and also lightly colour the bottom of the posts and the bottom bar of the gate.

10) Stage One of the embroidery is the cow parsley on either side of the gate in front of the fence.

11) Stage Two of the embroidery is the grasses along the fence line.

12) Stage Three is the final details on the front grass, a few French Knots along the grass and some small stitches where the gate would open for wear marks.

13) Take the other piece of white cotton and press the interfacing on the back. Pin this to the Postcard and zig zag round, cut off the excess fabric and then zig zag a number of times, making the stitch wider and tighter together, till you are happy with the finished edge.

Walk in the English country side and you come across lots of gates, this postcard is not based on one place but a lot of ideas put together, those fields that you follow the footpaths towards the next gate.

This postcard was inspired by a visit to a National Trust estate. The owners in the Victorian times had gone with this interesting metal gate all round the Estate, in the garden and also around the farms.

This postcard was inspired by a gate at the side of a trackway, it was set into a dry stone wall, with plants and mosses growing on the top. The gate was held shut with a loop of rope.

This gate is a more ornamental style one that I saw going into a field.

This postcard and gate were inspired by Wakehurst Place the country home of Kew. The gate was set into a hedge and led from the more formal area into the fields beyond. I chose to embroider the gate and also the metal sculptures.

Detailed Template for Field Gate

Cutting Template for Field Gate

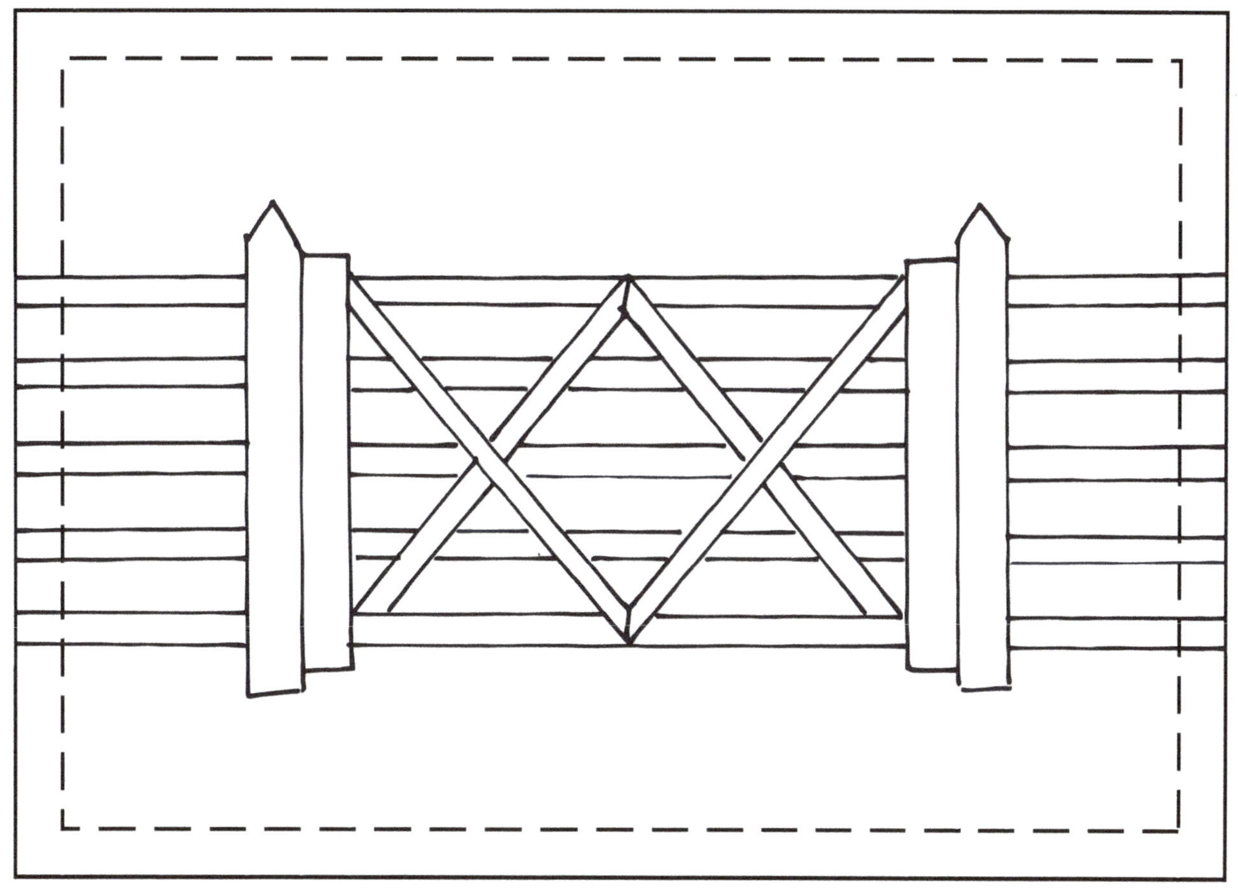

Shed

The first shed postcard was created for my Father-in-law's birthday, his man-shed was the inspiration. Since that first one I have gone on to create sheds in different forms, from garden ones to beach huts and a Bothy type shed.

You will need to make this Postcard

3 pieces of white cotton fabric 4½" x 6½"

2 pieces of iron-on interfacing 4½" x 6½"

1 piece of wadding 4" x 6"

Fusible Web

A selection of fabrics

A selection of sewing threads

A selection of stranded embroidery threads

Pigma Micron Archival Pen

Air erasable pen & Chalk pencils

1) Select the fabrics for the sky, hedging, gravel, shed, window, potting table and pots.

I have chosen small pattern fabrics for the sky, hedge and gravel. The fabric for the hedge had a directional print and so I placed it going vertical to give the feel of growing upwards. For the shed I chose a plain fabric to show the details.

2) Take the fusible web and then trace all the pieces onto it.

3) Cut the pieces out of the fusible web with a small allowance all round.

4) Press the fusible web onto the wrong side of the chosen fabrics.

5) Cut the pieces out on the marked line.

6) Take one piece of the white cotton fabric and press one piece of interfacing on the back.

7) Working on the cotton side, peel the backing paper off the sky, hedging, shed, window and gravel. Place the sky down first and then the shed, tucking the square for the window behind and also the hedging along the sides, then place down the gravel, press in place. Then peel the backing paper off the pieces for the table and pots and put them in place and press. Draw a 4" x 6" rectangle on the front.

8) Draw on the stitching lines for the door, window frame and roof.

9) Layer with the wadding and a piece of white cotton.

10) Stitch all the pieces and details and round the marked rectangle.

11) With the Micron pen mark the boarding on the shed and colour in the window and door frame.

12) Stage one of the embroidery is the rose stem up the side of the shed.

13) Stage two of the embroidery is the leaves on the rose.

14) Stage three of the embroidery is the flowers on the rose.

15) Stage four of the embroidery is the wreath on the door.

I used a small shirt button to draw a circle on the door, which I have then embroidered with a combination of green, white and variegated pink thread and French Knots.

16) Stage five of the embroidery is the plants in the pots.

For the pot on the table I have used two strands of green, I stitched the French Knots first, then the stems. The flowers are in two strands of variegated pink and Lazy Daisy Stitch. The plant in the pot under the table is stitched using two strands of a darker green and Lazy Daisy Stitch.

17) Stage six of the embroidery is the plants on the gravel.

I have stitched using two strands and long stitch some grass on the right hand side of the shed. Then using one strand and three twists round the needle I have stitched French Knots along the front of the shed. I then stitched random tiny stitches across the gravel in a muted green and a soft stone to add interest.

18) Press the interfacing to the back of the last piece of white cotton and then pin to the back of the postcard. Zig Zag round, cut off the excess fabric and then zig zag a number of times, making the stitch wider and tighter together, till you are happy with the finished edge.

This beach hut shed was one of the very early sheds I created, walking along the front of many seaside towns and the basic garden shed has been used as a beach hut, the beads I used to decorate the sand were from a bracelet bead kit Laura had as a young child and worked so well for this postcard.

A garden shed with flowers up the side and a window box full of blooms, this was another early version of the shed postcard.

The inspiration for this shed with a front porch area with roses growing up it, was the idea of a lovely craft shed at the end of the garden.

This version the shed has been turned into a stone bothy with a strong wooden door and window frame. The roof has plants growing on it and moss is in the crevasses in the wall.

Detailed Template for Shed

Cutting Template for Shed

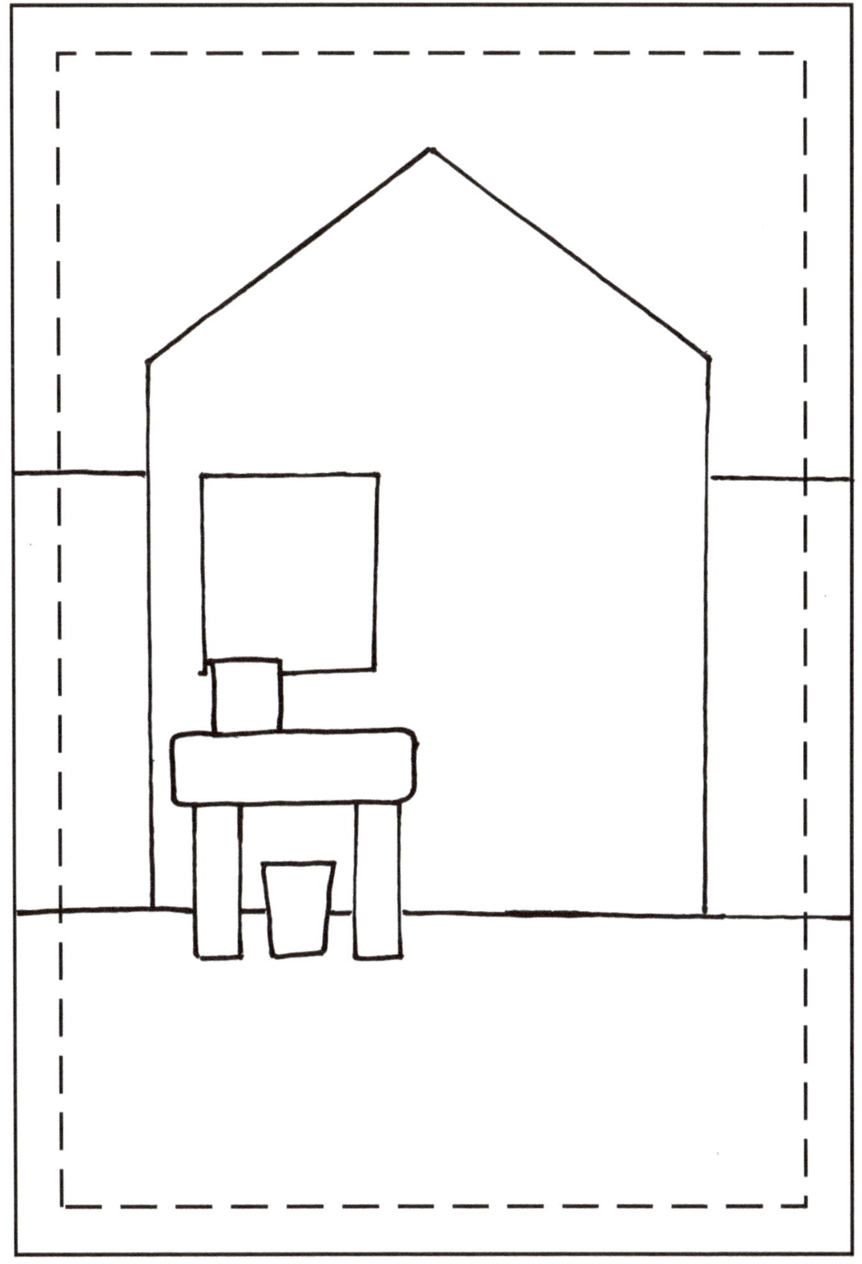

Just a reminder, all you need to do is to lay the fusible web, paper side up, onto this template and draw on the design. The template is already in mirror image.

Window & Balcony

Balconies and window boxes aren't so much an English thing but something you see on the Continent. I can remember visiting Bavaria, Austria and Switzerland as a child and the wooden chalets with masses of red geraniums in the window boxes in the alpine areas. In recent years I have noticed the balconies in cities with their flowers. All inspiration for me!!!

You will need to make this Postcard

2 pieces of white cotton fabric 4½" x 6½"

2 pieces of iron-on interfacing 4½" x 6½"

1 piece of wadding 4" x 6"

Fusible Web

A selection of fabrics

A selection of sewing threads

A selection of stranded embroidery threads

1) Select the fabrics, for the wall, doors & glass, balcony railings & the containers.

I have chosen a tone-on-tone fabric for the wall and cut it 4½" x 6½", white for the door frames and a pale grey with a squiggly pattern for the glass. The railings and bottom container are in blues and then I have gone with a mottled pink for the top containers, those hanging over the railing.

2) Take the fusible web and the trace the door frame, glass, balcony and containers, the bottom container runs all the way behind the railings and is one piece, onto it.

3) Cut the pieces out of the fusible web with a small seam allowance all round.

4) Press the fusible web onto the wrong side of the chosen fabrics.

5) Cut the pieces out on the marked line.

6) Press one piece of the interfacing to the back of the 4½" x 6½" piece of fabric for the wall.

7) Starting with the glass and door frame, peel the backing paper off the pieces and build up the design, followed by the bottom container, then the balcony and finally the top containers, carefully press the pieces in place. Draw a 4" x 6" rectangle on the front.

8) Layer with the wadding and a piece of white cotton.

9) Stitch all the pieces and round the marked rectangle.

All the stitching on this postcard is in straight stitch in matching thread to those being stitched. I started with the inner edges of the door frame and then the outer ones, the bottom container doesn't get stitched as it is behind the balcony, all the edges of this are stitched. The final stitching is the top containers.

10) Stage One of the embroidery is the daffodil plants in the bottom container.

11) Stage Two of the embroidery is the climbing plants coming from the bottom container

12) Stage Three of the embroidery is the evergreen tree (conifer) in the centre top container.

13) Stage Four of the embroidery is the tall plants in the top containers.

14) Stage Five of the embroidery is the trailing plants in the container.

15) Press the interfacing to the back of the last piece of white cotton and then pin to the back of the postcard. Zig zag round, cut off the excess fabric and then zig zag a number of times, making the stitch wider and tighter together, till you are happy with the finished edge.

Think of the balconies of France or Italy and this is the inspiration behind this postcard, with its stone walls and ironwork balustrade and plenty of plants and even a small tree.

National Trust properties are a huge source of inspiration, quirky buildings, with interesting doors or in this case window surrounded by old fashioned pink and white climbing roses.

These four postcards were made as a
series, one for each season. Spring
with dwarf Narcissus and the purple of
Grape hyacinths. Summer was a riot
of colour and lots of plants. Autumn
with cyclamen. Finally the Winter one
with a dwarf conifer and winter
berries on the plants.

I had been thinking of doing a window with shutters for a while, then I
came across the red fabric in my stash, it was perfect for the shutters and
luckily was just enough. I decided the window box needed to be in red,
white and blue theme to complement the shutters.

Detailed Template for Window & Balcony

Cutting Template for Window & Balcony

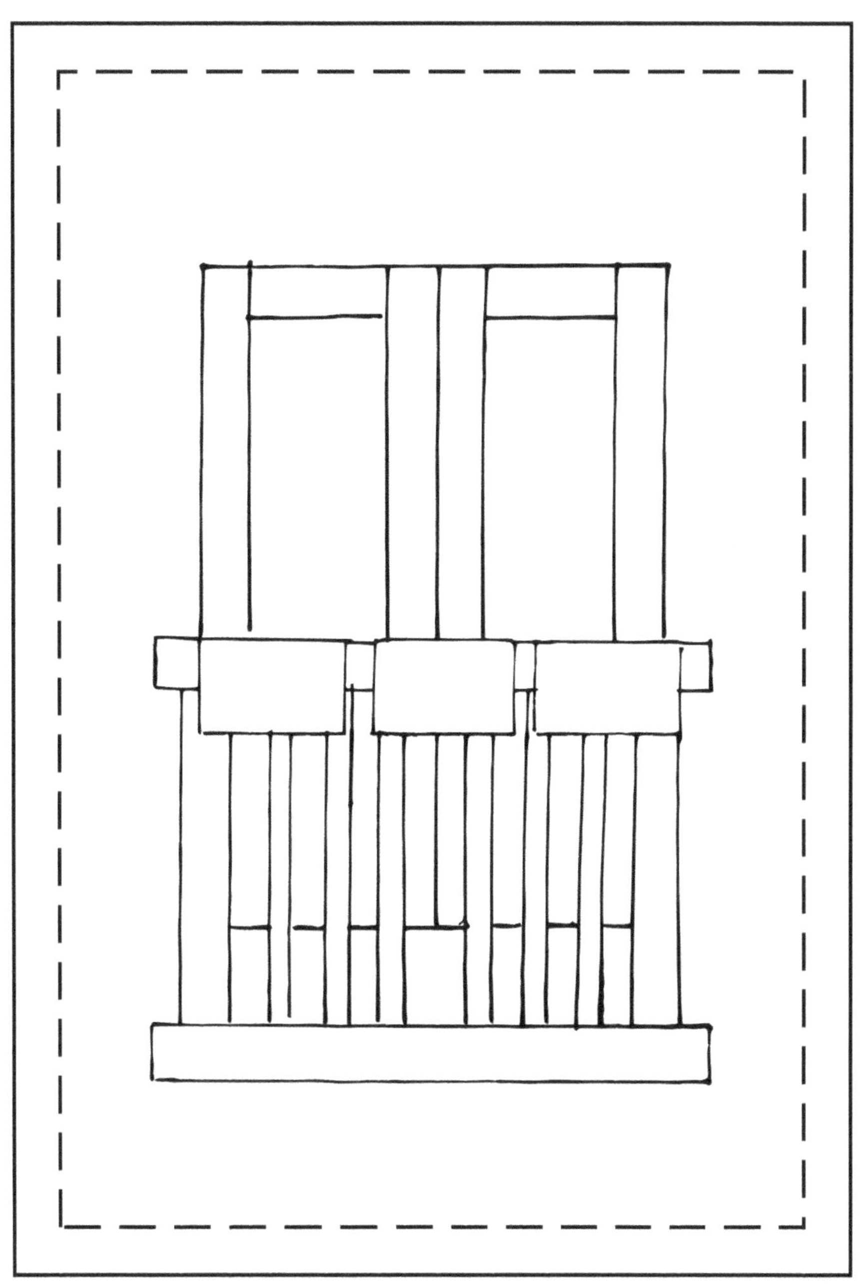

Landscape

My main inspiration for my landscape postcards is the English countryside from the West Country headlands to the Peak District, that we go on holiday to. I love dry stone walls, each district has a different way of building them!!! They are so interesting with the stones, mosses and plants that grow around them.

<table>
<tr><td>

You will need to make this Postcard

</td><td>

3 pieces of white cotton fabric 4½" x 6½"

2 pieces of iron-on interfacing 4½" x 6½"

1 piece of wadding 4" x 6"

Fusible Web

A selection of fabrics

A selection of sewing threads

A selection of stranded embroidery threads

Pigma Micron Archival Pen

Air erasable pen & Chalk pencils

</td></tr>
</table>

1) Select the fabrics for the sky, fields and wall.

> Mostly when I am creating dry-stone walls I will go with mottled fabric but for this postcard I have used a plain grey one. With the sky I have used the wrong side of this blue mottled fabric, the right side is a lot brighter, but the wrong side is a softer blue, I often do this with fabric.

2) Take the fusible web and then trace all the pieces.

3) Cut the pieces out of the fusible web with a small allowance all round.

4) Press the fusible web onto the wrong side of the chosen fabrics.

5) Cut the pieces out on the marked lines.

6) Take one piece of white cotton fabric and press one piece of the interfacing on the back.

7) Working on the cotton side, peel the backing paper off all the pieces, lay the sky down first and then build up the landscape from the top down. Press a the pieces in place. Draw a 4" x 6" rectangle on the front.

8) Layer with the wadding and a piece of white cotton.

9) Stitch all the pieces and details and round the marked rectangle.

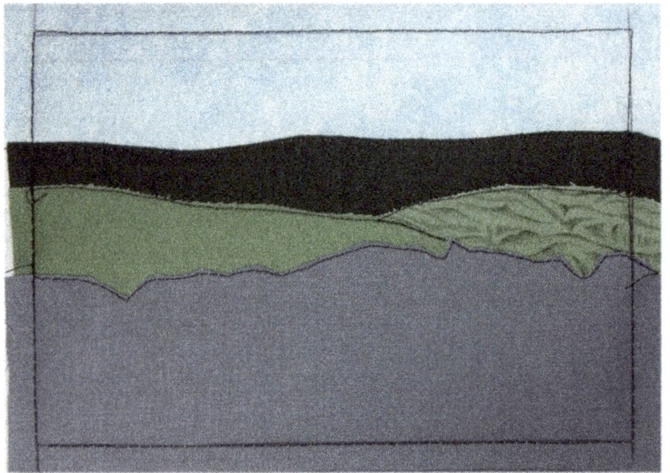

10) Draw the stones on the wall.

11) Stage one of the embroidery is the stitching on the hills and fields.

12) Stage two of the embroidery is the grasses at the front.

13) Stage three of the embroidery is the moss on the wall.

14) Press the interfacing to the back of the last piece of white cotton and then pin to the back of the postcard. Zig Zag round, cut off the excess fabric and then zig zag a number of times, making the stitch wider and tighter together, till you are happy with the finished edge.

This is another postcard inspired by the Peak District, we dropped down off the footpath onto a lane through a village and built into the dry-stone wall was a post box, the wall was in a shady spot and had lots of mosses covering it. I knew as soon as I saw it that I wanted to create a postcard inspired by it!

Inspirations

On a walk in the Peak District you will find piles of stones, often on cairns at the top of tors and also in smaller piles where people have stopped to sit, rest and look at the views across the valleys to the next peak.

Dry-stone walls aren't just used for field boundaries, often in villages they are built from local stone as front garden walls, this postcard is inspired by them and the flower beds that are often against them.

I will often take photos of the plants that grow along the dry stone walls from cow parsley, foxgloves to the simple grasses and this postcard is inspired by those plants.

This landscape of an estuary was inspired by Rock in Cornwall, looking across the water to the hills beyond with the plants in the foreground.

Another postcard inspired by the coastline, this time it was a walk along the Devon coastline above Croyde looking across a wall, with its dry grasses and flowering sea thrift, across the misty headland.

Detailed Template for Landscape

Cutting Template for Landscape

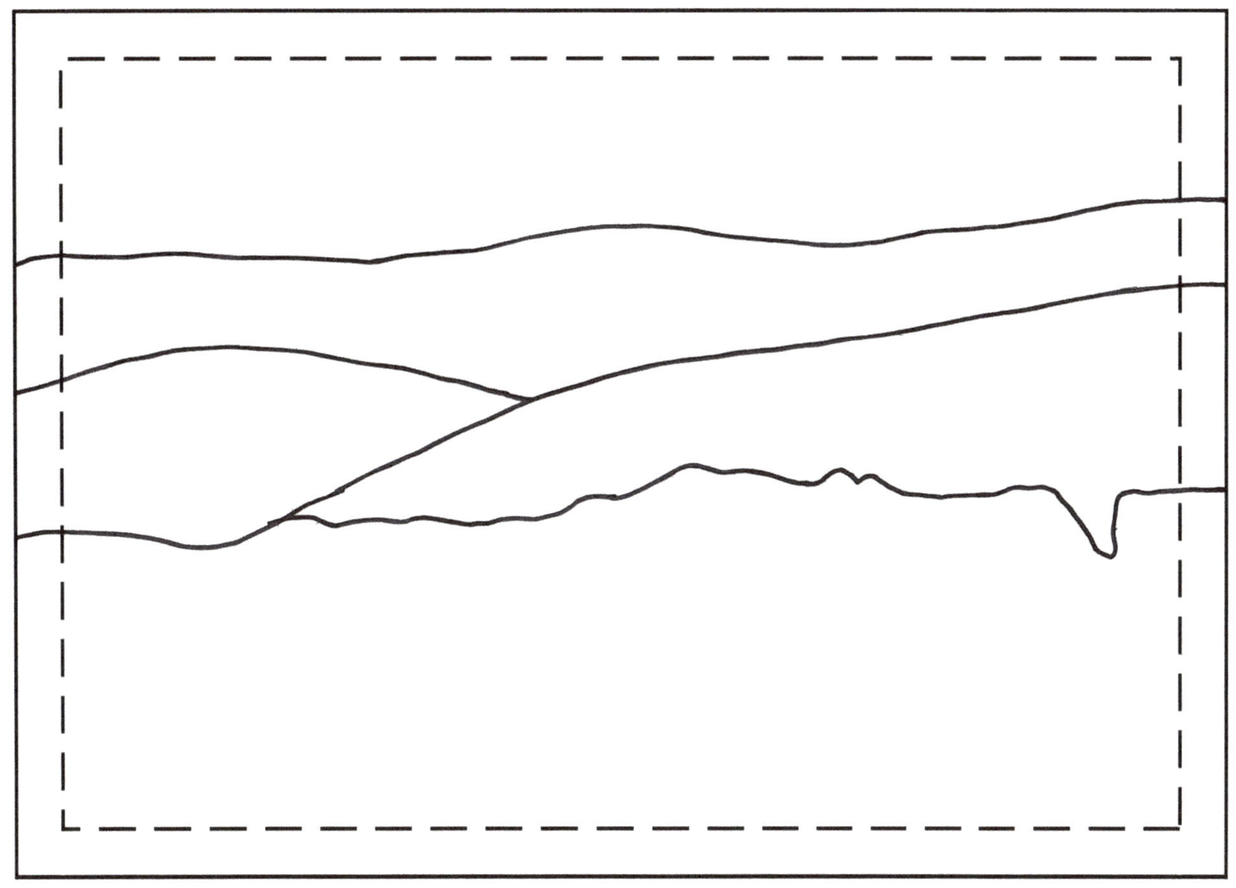

Porch & Door

The idea for the first of the Porch & Door postcards was from reading a magazine and a picture of the quintessential cottage door with porch and rambling roses all round it. But it was winter, and I wanted a Christmas Postcard and so it had Christmas wreath and garland. I then challenged myself to make one postcard a month for the year, in the end I made a Bakers dozen in the series!

You will need to make this Postcard

2 pieces of white cotton fabric 4½" x 6½"

2 pieces of iron-on interfacing 4½" x 6½"

1 piece of wadding 4" x 6"

Fusible Web

A selection of fabrics

A selection of sewing threads

A selection of stranded embroidery threads

Micron Archival pen

Air erasable pen & Chalk pencils

1) Select the fabric, a piece 4 ½" x 6 ½" for the background and then brown for the porch, stone for the pots and a fabric for the front door.

The fabric for the background is the colour of the wall and also the paving in front and so I have used a soft tone on tone sandy colour. The brown for the porch has a slight shading in it. I have chosen a muted blue for the door.

2) Take the fusible web and the trace the pieces for the porch, door and pots onto it.

3) Cut the pieces out of the fusible web with a small allowance all round.

4) Press the fusible web onto the wrong side of the chosen fabrics.

5) Cut the pieces out on the marked lines.

6) Take the background fabric and press one piece of the interfacing on the back.

7) Working on the cotton side, peel the backing paper off all the pieces, put the door in place first and then the porch and pots, press in place when happy with the placement. Draw a 4" x 6" rectangle on the front.

8) Draw on the stitching lines on the door and front of the porch.

9) Layer with the wadding and a piece of white cotton.

10) Stitch all the pieces and details and round the marked rectangle.

I start with stitching the door and I have used a shade darker thread than the fabric and straight stitch. For the porch I stitched it all in a dark grey, straight stitch round the edges and the details. For the roof I stitch a narrow close together zig zag, I start at the top point and go down one edge and back up, then down the other and back up, I then go round the zig zag with straight stitch. The plant pots I have used a matching thread and blanket stitch.

11) Stage one of the embroidery is the stem of the rose.

I have embroidered the stem with two different threads together, one of a dark green and the other a dark brown, to give an older woody effect.

12) Stage two of the embroidery is the leaves on the rose.

I have used a combination of three different shades of green thread, two strands of thread, in the individual shades and also mixing them together and individual Lazy Daisy Stitch for the leaves.

13) Stage three of the embroidery is the
flowers on the rose.

14) Stage four of the embroidery is the
wreath on the door.

I often find myself embroidering the flowers on roses in either pink or white as these are my favourite shades for roses, I decided to do this one in yellow, I mixed a plain yellow with a variegated one, and used two strands and two or three twists for the French Knots.

Using the air erasable pen I marked the middle line of the door for the ribbon and then drew round a small shirt button for the circle for the wreath. I keep a number of different size shirt buttons just for drawing round for things like wreaths and flower centres. I embroidered the wreath in two strands of green and then two strands of a variegated yellow, which I also used for the ribbon.

15) Stage five of the embroidery is the flowering plant in the pot.

16) Stage six of the embroidery is the trailing plants spilling out of the top of the pots.

17) Draw the handle on the door with the Micron Archival pen.

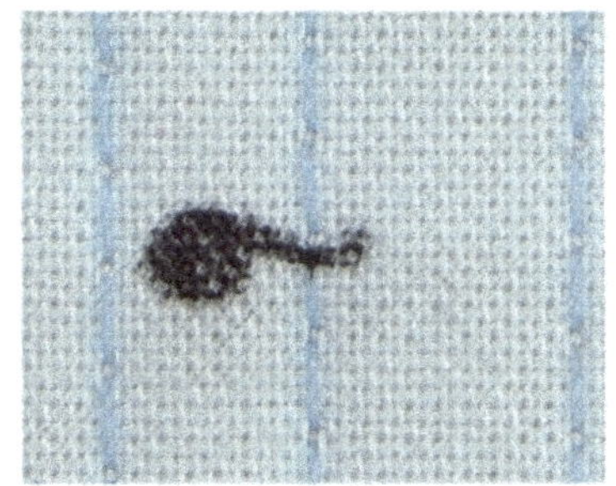

18) Press the interfacing to the back of the last piece of white cotton and then pin to the back of the postcard. Zig Zag round, cut off the excess fabric and then zig zag a number of times, making the stitch wider and tighter together, till you are happy with the finished edge.

Inspirations

Here are the 13 Porch & Door Postcards that I made over the course of a year. It started with Christmas and then one for each month after that. While the designs are all very much the same, I have added details that are specific to the month, like the flowers or the wreath.

It also shows just how different size each one finishes up as despite all starting the same size. The joy of working with fabric!

Cutting Template for Porch & Door

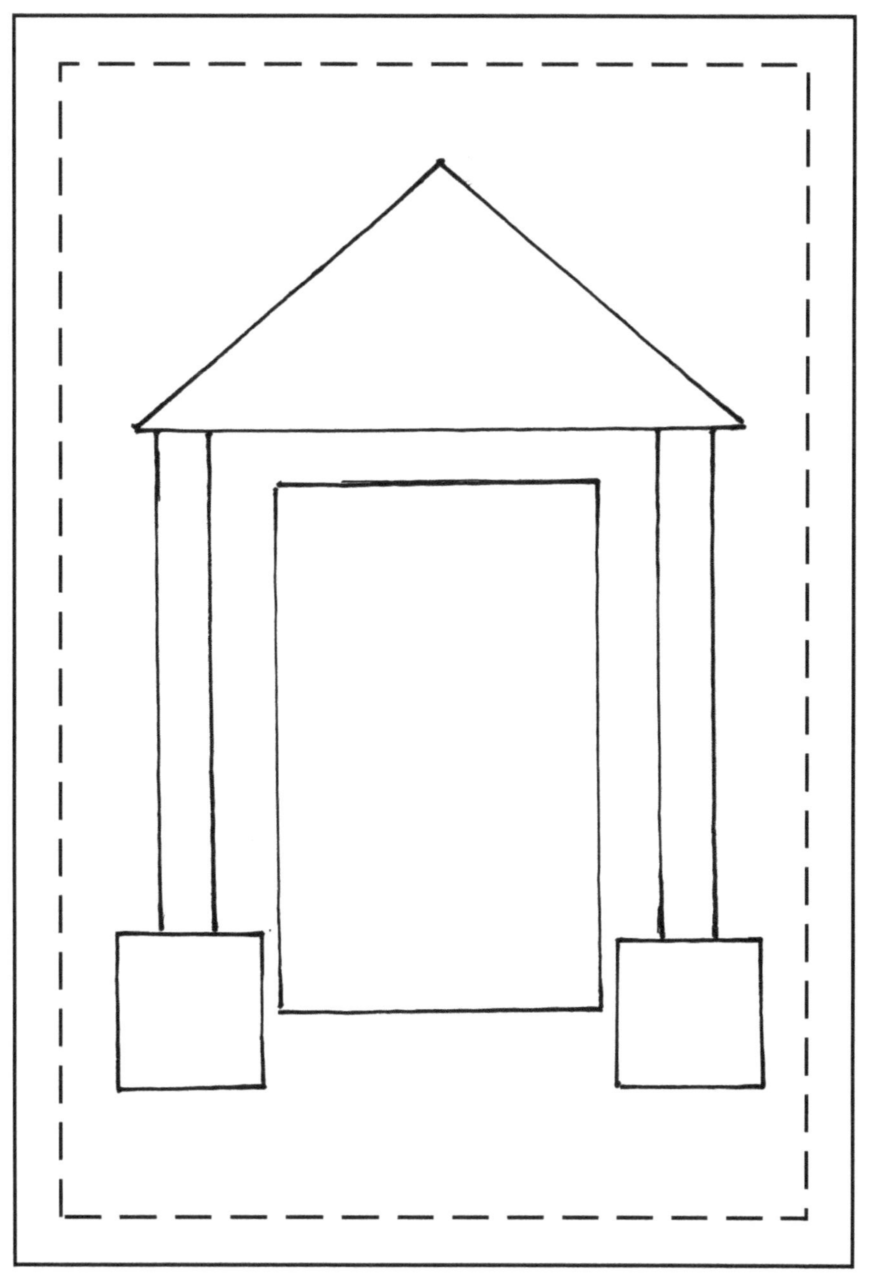

Wrought Iron Gate

The first few wrought iron gates were inspired by front garden gates locally, then I started looking online for a replacement back gate for us and I found wealth of inspiration!!! From manufacturers catalogues to artisan creators there are so many different gates and they have become a bit of an obsession!!!

You will need to make this Postcard

3 pieces of white cotton fabric 4½" x 6½"

2 pieces of iron-on interfacing 4½" x 6½"

1 piece of wadding 4" x 6"

Fusible Web

A selection of fabrics

A selection of sewing threads

A selection of stranded embroidery threads

Pigma Micron Archival Pen

Air erasable pen

1) Select the fabrics for the sky, walls, hedge and grass and gravel.

I have chosen two tone on tone greens for beyond the gate to look like a hedge and grass, using tone on tone adds interest but not too much. I prefer mottled fabrics for walls and with this postcard I have gone with a grey tone one.

2) Take the fusible web and the trace all the pieces on.

3) Cut the pieces out of the fusible web with a small allowance all round.

4) Press the fusible web onto the wrong side of the chosen fabrics.

5) Cut the pieces out on the marked lines.

6) Take one piece of white cotton fabric and press one piece of the interfacing on the back.

7) Working on the cotton side, peel the backing paper off all the pieces, place the sky down first, then the hedge and grass, followed by the gravel and finally the walls, press in place. Draw a 4" x 6" rectangle on the front.

8) Layer with the wadding and a piece of white cotton.

9) Stitch all the pieces and details and round the marked rectangle.

I always put the wall pieces in place and then measure with a acrylic ruler, that the gap is even all the way down & that the walls line up on the bottom and are straight to the gravel. I think things are straight but when I measure, I find they aren't. Once I am sure they are straight and even, then I press them in place.

The stitching is simple on this postcard, I use straight stitch and matching thread on the hedge, grass and gravel and then I have used blanket stitch round the walls.

10) Using an air erasable pen draw on the gate and then when happy go over with the Micron Archival pen.

12) Stage two of the embroidery is the stem of the climbing rose.

11) Stage one of the embroidery is the gate.

13) Stage three of the embroidery is the leaves on the rose.

14) Stage four of the embroidery is the flowers on the rose.

15) Stage five of the embroidery is the plants along the base of the wall.

16) Press the interfacing to the back of the last piece of white cotton and then pin to the back of the postcard. Zig Zag round, cut off the excess fabric and then zig zag a number of times, making the stitch wider and tighter together, till you are happy with the finished edge.

When I saw this design in a catalogue I knew I would have to make it into a postcard! I loved the curls and leaves at the bottom, I have stitched a hydrangea on the right hand side.

This garden gate caught my eye, it took the traditional wrought iron front gate and made it new and current.

These four just are a few of the gates I have created, there are so many designs from traditional to modern artisan gates out there to take for inspiration.

I just loved the idea of a spiders web gate, I have used variations of this design for an autumn/Halloween design and also for a moon gate. I love looking at the webs in our garden in the autumn with the dew clinging to them making them beautiful.

The inspiration for this postcard was a traditional Victorian front garden gate that led to steps and eventually to a substantial Victorian Villa with wrought iron balconies, in a spa town.

Detailed Template for Wrought Iron Gate

Cutting Template for Wrought Iron Gate

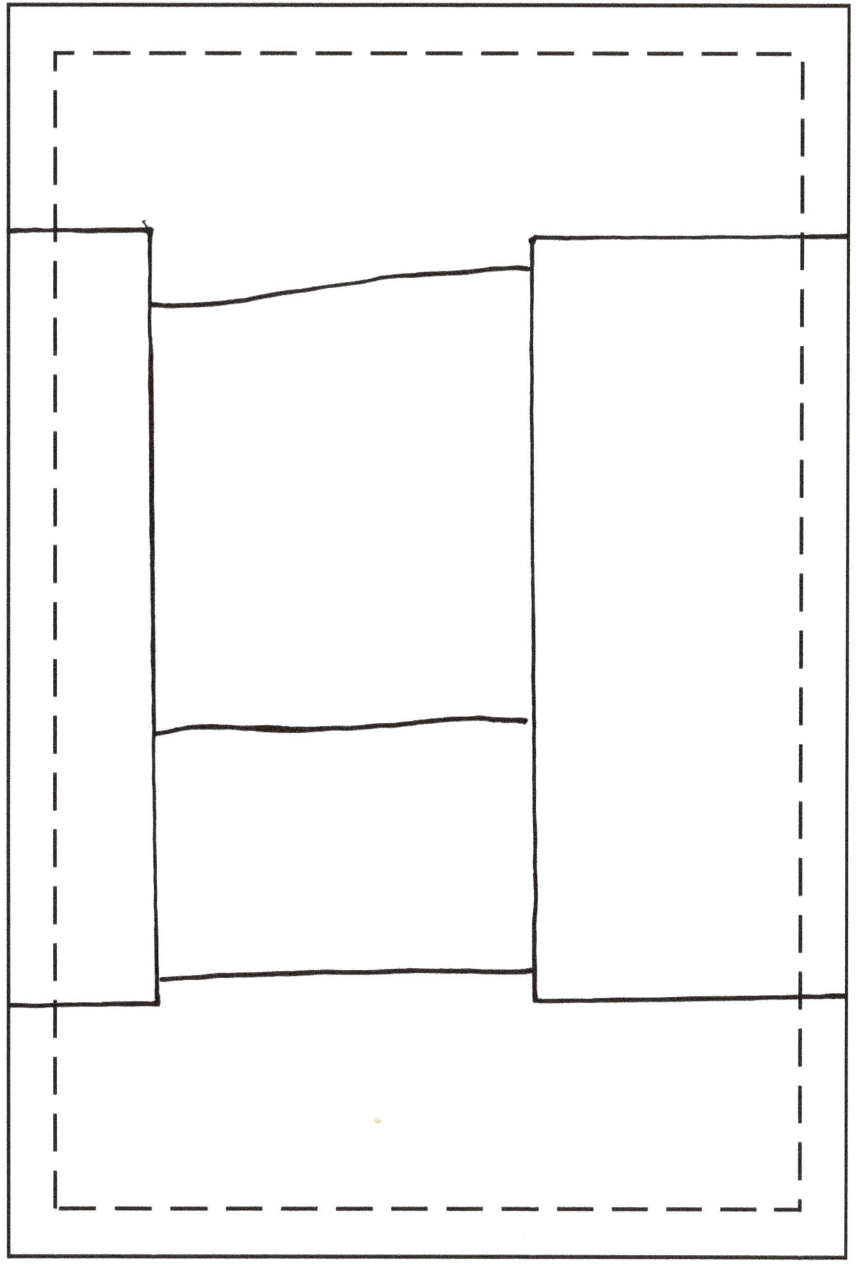

Just a reminder, all you need to do is to lay the fusible web, paper side up, onto this template and draw on the design. The template is already in mirror image.

Moon Gate

I came across a photo of a Moon Gate in a gardening book a number of years ago, I had never heard of them before that and suddenly I was on a journey of discovery, and I fell in love with the design possibilities. The first Moon Gate I created in fabric was in a bigger format - a journal (A4) size but then I started making them in Quilted Postcard size and haven't stopped!

You will need to make this Postcard

3 pieces of white cotton fabric 4½" x 6½"

2 pieces of iron-on interfacing 4½" x 6½"

1 piece of wadding 4" x 6"

Fusible web

A selection of fabrics

A selection of sewing threads

A selection of stranded embroidery threads

Pigma Archival Pen

Air erasable pen

1) Select the fabrics for the sky, gravel, pot, wall and Moon Gate.

I have gone with bright summer blue for the sky, the gravel, pot, wall and Moon Gate are all in very similar shades of light stone fabric.

2) Take the fusible web and trace all the design pieces onto it and cut out with a small seam allowance all round.

3) Press the fusible web onto the wrong side of the chosen fabric.

4) Cut out the pieces on the marked lines.

5) Take one piece of the white cotton fabric and press one piece of interfacing on the back.

6) Working on the cotton side, peel the backing paper off the sky, walls and gravel and arrange on the white cotton. When happy with the placement, press in place. Peel the paper backing off the pot, place on top of the gravel section. When happy with the placement, press. Draw a 4" x 6" rectangle on the front.

7) Layer with the wadding and a piece of white cotton fabric.

8) Machine applique all the pieces.

9) Using an Air erasable pen I drew the lines on both the wall and Moon Gate. I then lightly drew in the bricks with a Micron Archival pen.

10) Stage One of the embroidery is the plants in the pot, a combination of straight stitches for the grasses and French Knots for the trailing small plants.

11) Stage Two of the embroidery is the plants at the base of the wall.

12) Stage Three is the grasses along the edge of the Moon Gate.

13) Stage Four of the embroidery is more French Knots under the grasses against the Moon Gate.

14) Take the other piece of white cotton and press the interfacing on the back. Pin this to the Postcard and zig zag round, cut off the excess fabric and then zig zag a number of times, making the stitch wider and tighter together, till you are happy with the finished edge.

Inspirations

This postcard was inspired by a photo in a magazine of an Oriental garden, with a wooden trellis screen. I created it as a Moon Gate with a flowering tree as the focal point.

I came across a spiders web gate design years ago, which I created as a basic gate postcard, then as a Halloween themed one and then I had the idea of taking the gate design and using it in a Moon Gate! I wanted it to have a feel of an autumn day and so decided to embroider a creeping vine like a Virginia creeper that gives beautiful colour in autumn around the Moon Gate.

Another Moon Gate in a garden, a beautiful York stone wall with the Moon Gate leading to a damp shady area with a hedge and evergreen shrubs and hostas. A cool quiet area to stop and reflect.

A Moon Gate in a wall, with a wrought iron gate leading to a field. This postcard combines two things I love and inspire me.

Moon Gates come in many forms and styles and the inspiration for this one was in a garden book. A wooden fence with the Moon Gate was the divide from one section of the garden through to another.

Detailed Template for Moon Gate

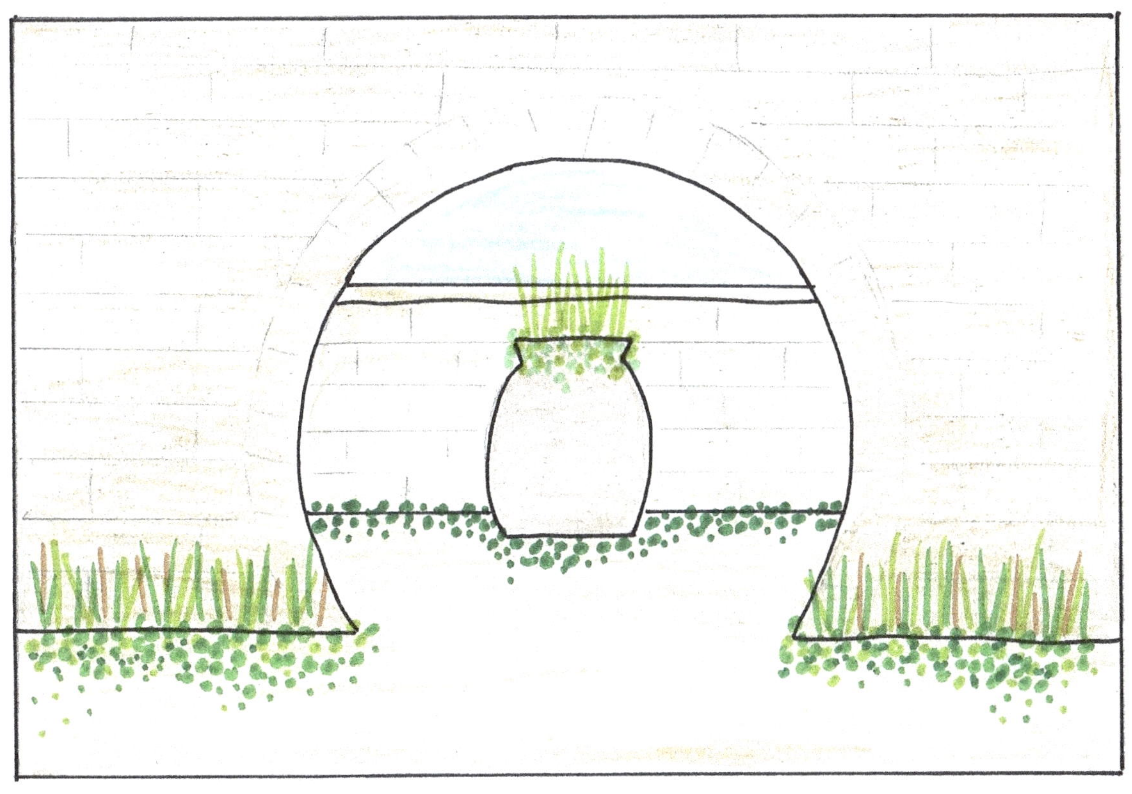

Cutting Template for Moon Gate

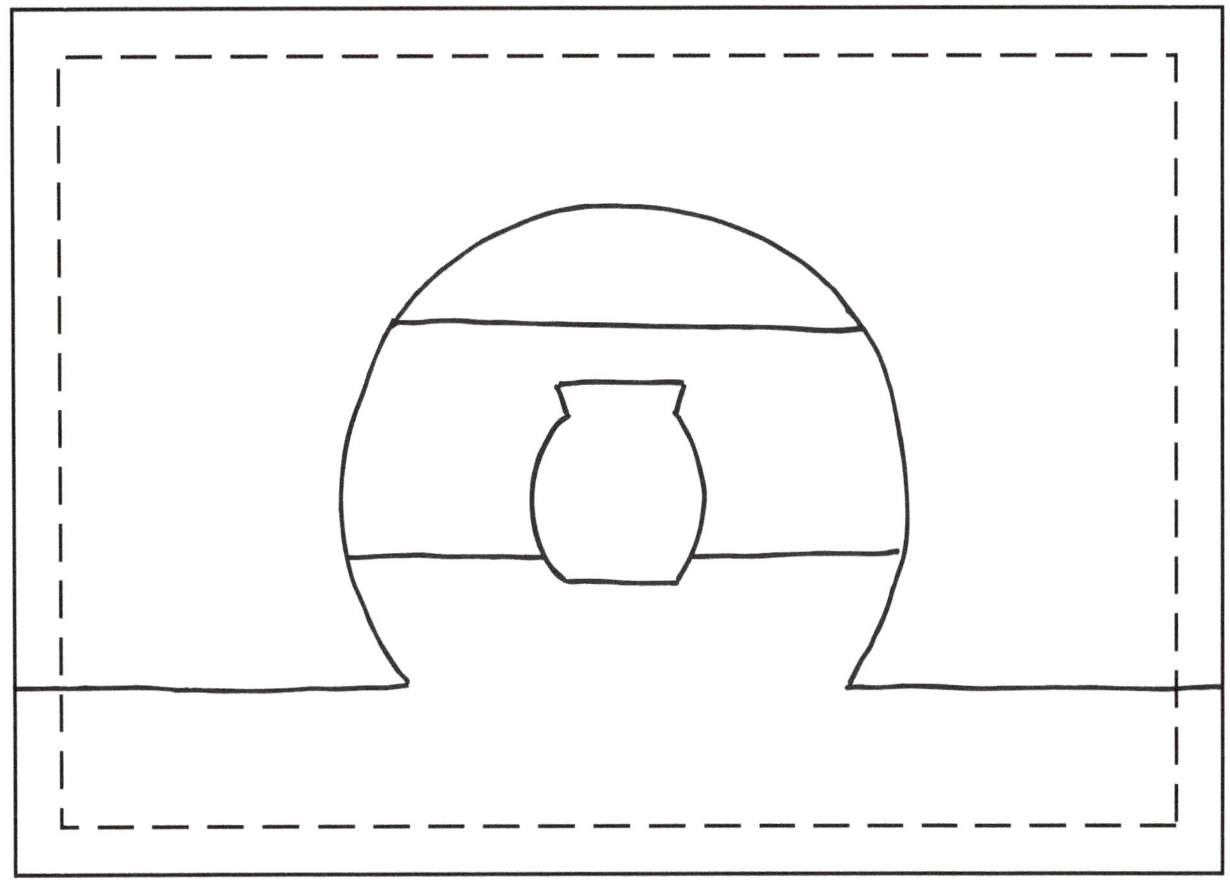

Sundial & Watering Can

My fascination with old watering cans started with a really old, galvanised steel one that we found in the overgrown garden when we moved into our Home, it's a bit battered but that adds to its charm. Since then, I have added another one, they aren't used, not as watering cans but as decorative pieces by the water features.

Old watering cans and sundials remind me of the gardens, especially the old walled gardens of Stately homes, as we wander around them its not unusual to find one or both of them.

You will need to make this Postcard

- 3 pieces of white cotton fabric 4½" x 6½"
- 2 pieces of iron-on interfacing 4½" x 6½"
- 1 piece of wadding 4" x 6"
- Fusible web
- A selection of fabrics
- A selection of sewing threads
- A selection of stranded embroidery threads
- Pigma Archival Pen
- Air erasable pen and chalk pencils

1) Select the fabrics for the sky, gravel, pots, sundial, and watering can.

I have gone with a deep green for my watering can, but you can go with any colour.

2) Take the fusible web and trace the pieces on the pot, sundial, planter and the watering can. The gravel is a 1¼" x 4½" rectangle and the sky is a 5¼" x 6½" rectangle.

With the gravel and sky I have added the seam allowances where needed.

3) Cut the pieces out of the fusible web with a small seam allowance all round.

4) Press the fusible web onto the wrong side of the chosen fabrics.

5) Cut the pieces out on the marked line.

6) Take one piece of the white cotton fabric and press one piece of interfacing on the back.

7) Working on the cotton side, peel the backing paper off the sky and gravel and place in position on the fabric, press in place. Peel the paper backing off the planter and sundial, place on top of the gravel section, when happy with the placement, press. Do the same for the watering can and pot. Draw a 4" x 6" rectangle on the fabric.

8) Using the chalk pencil & air erasable pen draw on the details onto the planter, pot, sundial and watering can.

9) Layer with the wadding and a piece of white cotton.

10) Stitch all the pieces and details and round the marked rectangle.

11) With a micron pen colour in the piece that creates the shadow on the top of the sundial and also the rivet on the handle of the watering can.

12) Stage One of embroidery is the taller flowers in the container.

13) Stage Two of the embroidery is the French knot trailing plants in the container.

14) Stage Three of the embroidery is the plant in the pot, the stems are worked in split stitch with Lazy Daisy Stitched leaves up each side of the stems, the flowers are French Knots.

15) Stage Four of the embroidery is the French Knots on the gravel at the base of the pot, those on the bottom of the sundial to look like moss and random little stitches in the gravel.

16) Press the interfacing to the back of the last piece of white cotton and then pin to the back of the postcard. Zig zag round, cut off the excess fabric and then zig zag a number of times, making the stitch wider and tighter together, till you are happy with the finished edge.

This postcard was inspired by a National Trust Garden. We wandered along a box bush lined path and at the intersection was a sundial on a big plinth surrounded by pots and planters, their flowers were all bright colours but when I came to making this postcard I chose to do an all-white theme.

Inspirations

This was inspired by the original galvanised steel watering can I have in the garden and a few of the many pots that I have dotted around. I mostly garden in pots and containers.

Often walking around Historic gardens we come across old watering cans just left, sometimes the plants have started to grow round them and climb up them and this is what I was trying to create with this postcard, nature taking over, with the flower climbing up the handle.

This postcard is another where I was trying to get that feel of nature taking over, with both the watering can and the sundial having plants climbing up them and they are disappearing under the plants.

Sundials are often at the ends of long walks in gardens and surrounded by greens of hedges or grass, or they are in formal gardens. This one is surrounded by plants and flowers in the middle of a border.

Detailed Template for Sundial & Watering Can

Cutting Template for Sundial & Watering Can

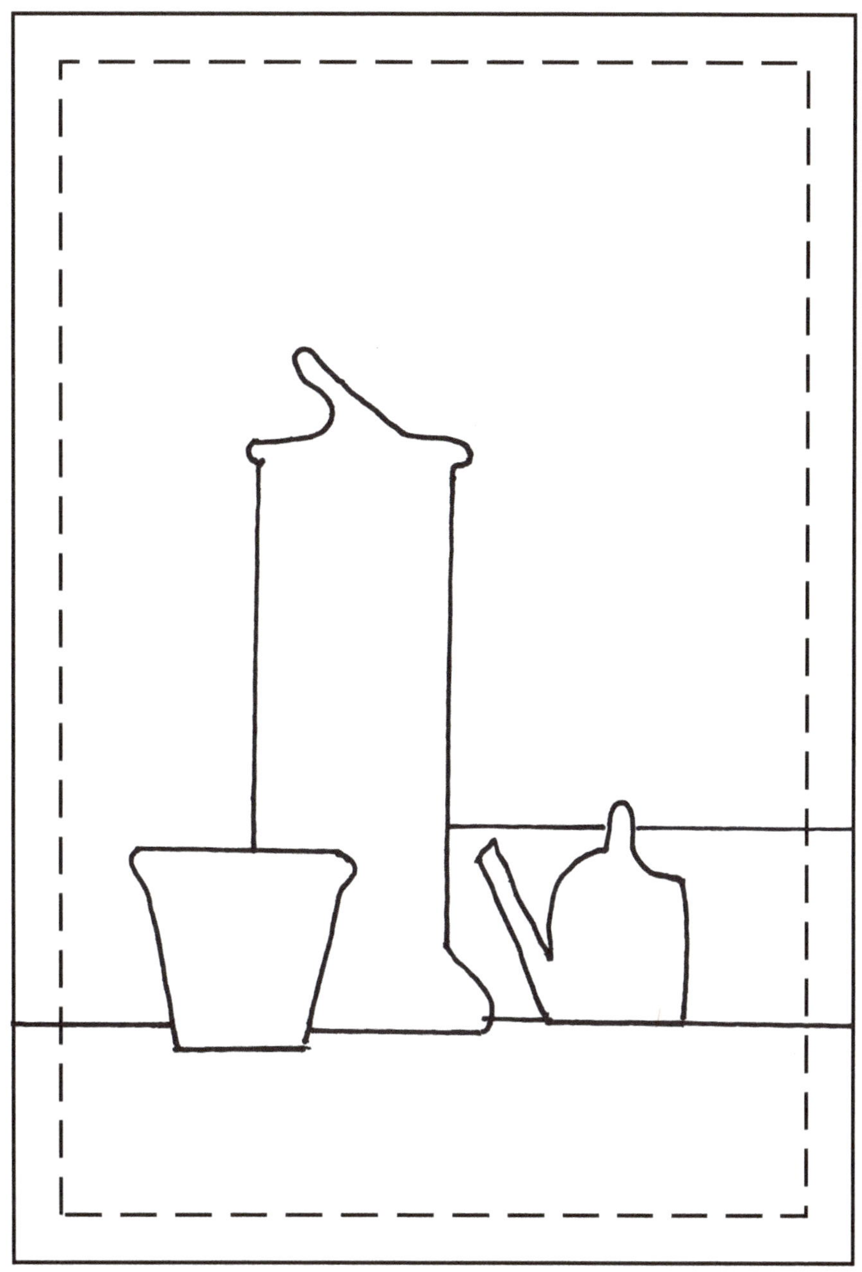

Just a reminder, all you need to do is to lay the fusible web, paper side up, onto this template and draw on the design. The template is already in mirror image.

Flowering Door

I was sent a Christmas card a long time ago with the front of a Regency house in a line drawing and then the decorations in colours. This was the starting point of my quilted front doors series, the doors are quilted and then flowers, garland, trees embroidered around them.

You will need to make this Postcard

2 pieces of white cotton fabric 4½" x 6½"

2 pieces of iron-on interfacing 4½" x 6½"

1 piece of wadding 4" x 6"

Fusible Web

A selection of fabrics

A selection of sewing threads

A selection of stranded embroidery threads

Pigma Micron Archival Pen

Air erasable pen & Chalk pencils

1) Select the fabric for the background of the postcard, this needs to be 4½" x 6½" and for the container.

For the background I have used a white on white small print fabric, I use these a lot in my quilt making and always have pieces around for postcards. Sometimes I use a plain white piece of cotton. For the container I have gone with a very bright pink for a splash of colour.

2) Take the fusible web and the trace the container (1" x 1¼") onto it.

3) Cut the piece out of the fusible web with a small allowance all round.

4) Press the fusible web onto the wrong side of the chosen fabric.

5) Cut the piece out on the marked lines.

6) Take the fabric for the background and press one piece of the interfacing on the back.

7) Draw a 4" x 6" rectangle on the front. Then peel the backing paper of the container and press in place.

8) Draw the front door onto the fabric using an erasable pen.

9) Layer with the wadding and a piece of white cotton.

10) Stitch the front door and the container and round the marked rectangle.

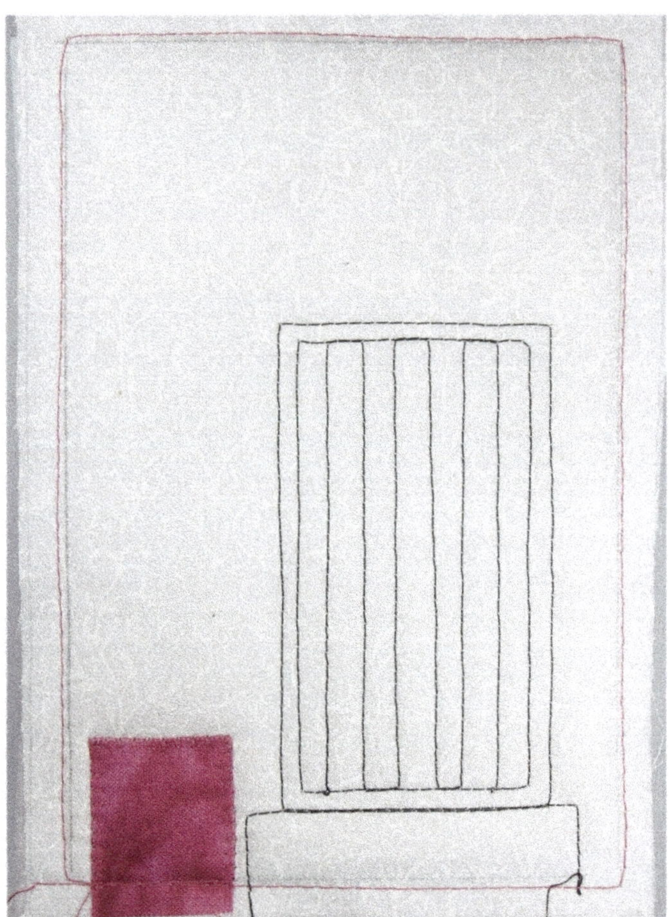

For the stitching of the front door I have used straight stitch and a very dark grey thread, Gutermann Sew all thread col 36, I prefer this to a black as its not as harsh. The container I have stitched in a matching thread and blanket stitch.

11) Stage one of the embroidery is the trunk and branches of the tree.

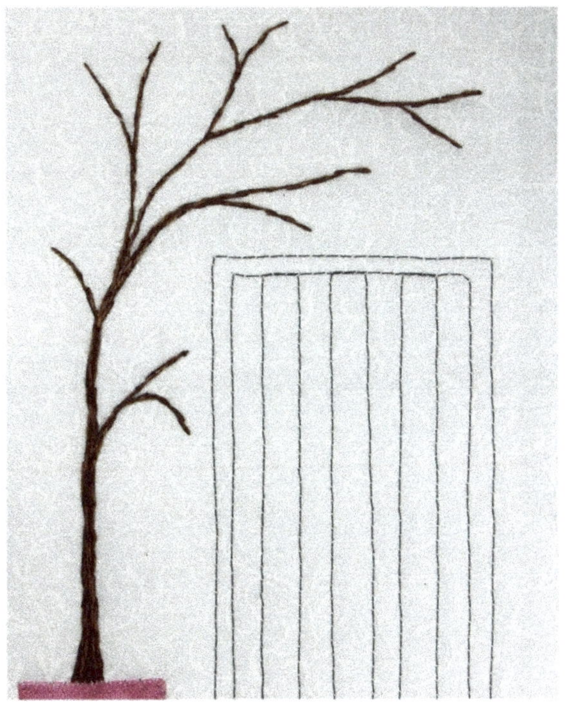

13) Stage three of the embroidery is the door handle.

12) Stage two of the embroidery is all the French Knots that create the blossom.

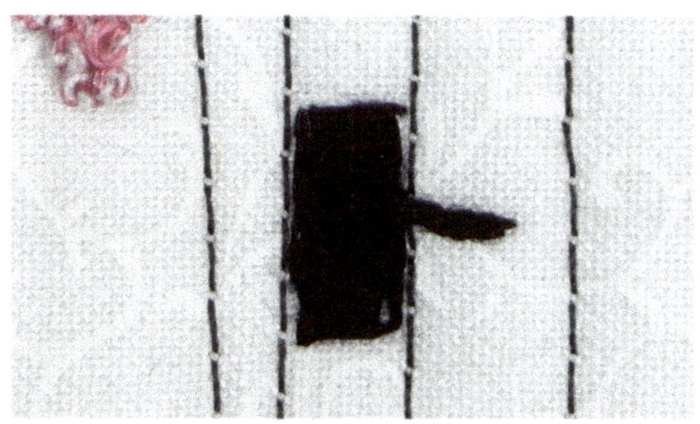

14) Press the interfacing to the back of the last piece of white cotton and then pin to the back of the postcard. Zig Zag round, cut off the excess fabric and then zig zag a number of times, making the stitch wider and tighter together, till you are happy with the finished edge.

This postcard was inspired by the wisteria growing round our porch and also by a huge one covering the front of a house near us, with their woody stems and masses of flowers.

I stitch a lot of rambling roses rounds gates and doors and so I just had to do it as a quilted door postcard, the French knot flowers are stitched using two different colour threads mixed together.

This postcard is just French Knots, hundreds of them, stitched in lots of soft pastel colours to represent a floral arch, often seen round shop doors in London.

I wanted to keep this postcard fairly simple, an arch of winter greenery with a traditional red and green wreath for a Christmas theme.

Detailed Template for Flowering Door

Cutting Template for Flowering Door

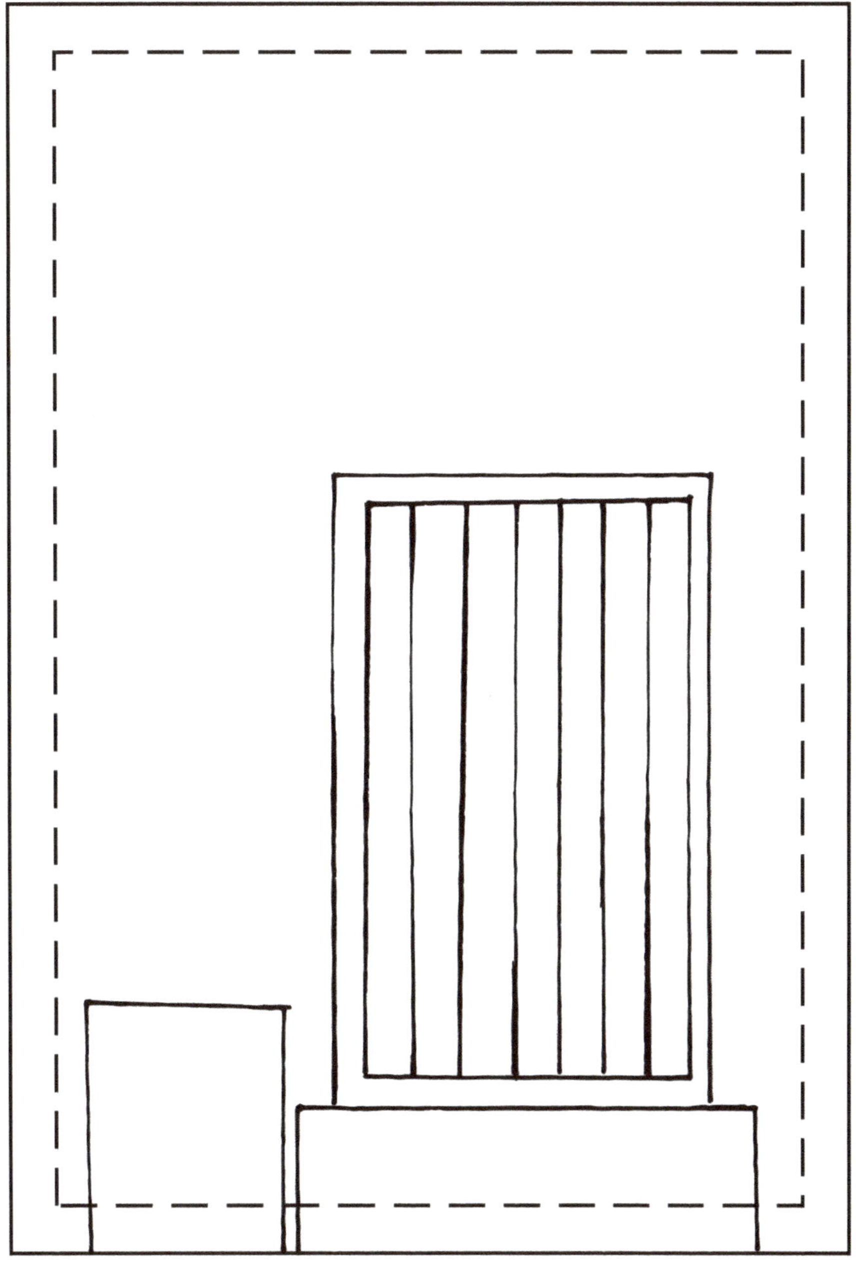

Just a reminder, the door is included on this template just so that it helps you to position the pot and for drawing the door!!

I fell in love with patchwork & quilting when I was nineteen years old in the late 1980's, since then I have been constantly learning new ideas and skills. I am completely self-taught, and I have no formal qualifications in any form of art, design, textiles, or the history of patchwork. My ethos is to create things that I enjoy making and love when finished and that anyone with basic sewing skills can also make and enjoy. My inspiration for my quilts is those made in the past, from English Paper Piecing, pieced Nine Patch Block to the quilting of the North Country.

Quilted Postcards are an offshoot of my quilt making. I made my first one in 2008, I was looking for something to replace the ties that I had been making for my husband, Tony, as presents. I saw an article on making postcards using pre-printed fabric designs. The idea of Quilted Postcards really appealed to me and so I began creating them – I started with the designs from the ties – just for Tony. Then for our daughter Laura. From there it has spread to family and friends and for all occasions. I create different types of Quilted Postcards from simple applique ones to the 'Arty' ones that this book is all about, a combination of machine applique, drawing and embroidery.

The Books

I have always dreamed of publishing a book, I used to be a bookseller!!! Quilted Postcards – Little Quilts of Creativity took years to come to fruition, I started it, and stopped and started again – life kept getting in the way, I almost gave up on it! But Tony and Laura kept nagging me and then along came 2020 – and we got it published.

After the first book, we knew that we had to do another one – I have far too many ideas and postcards, so we created the second book Quilted Postcards – The Flower Edition and then of course we had to do The Christmas Edition and now this fourth book.

The Tortoise Logo

As a child on holiday in Yorkshire, I can remember going to a museum/workshop of a furniture maker. He carved a mouse into all his creations, and that was all I could remember about visiting there!!! The idea stuck with me, so when I was looking for a logo to 'stamp' on to my postcards, using a tortoise just came to mind.

The tortoise has been a very long running joke between Tony and I. I'm very happy staying at home, in my shell just creating. I am a tortoise!!! When I drew up my tortoise, I knew she couldn't be a plain, ordinary shelled one, she had a have a patchwork of colours and be wearing a scarf and carrying a bag with her knitting (I also crochet and weave!!!)

(PS, the furniture maker was Robert Thompson).

The Internet & Tortoise Crafts

www.tortoisecrafts.co.uk is the digital home of both Quilted Postcards 'Little Quilts of Creativity' and Tortoise Crafts – the rest of the creativity that I do, basically anything to do with fabric, fibre or threads and occasionally gardening!!! Since 2020 it has expanded to include the stitcheries that Laura does, we have a range of Blackwork embroidery patterns that are available through our Etsy store.

I don't blog but I 'Ramble' - my version of a blog!!! And these can be found on my website. They get written on a semi-regular basis and they can wander/ramble off in any direction. There are also *Free Patterns* available on the website, as well as stories about my quilts and quilt making.

I also regularly post on Facebook and Instagram, showing what I am working on and what is inspiring me to create and hopefully inspiring others.

Sarah

My first 3 books are available on Amazon or available to order from your local book shop.

Quilted Postcards—Little Quilts Of Creativity

Quilted Postcards—The Flower Edition

Quilted Postcards—The Christmas Edition

Social Media

You can find me on:

www.tortoisecrafts.co.uk

www.facebook.com/tortoisecrafts/

www.instagram.com/tortoisecrafts/

www.youtube.com/@tortoisecrafts

www.pinterest.com/tortoisecraftsuk

www.etsy.com/uk/shop/TortoiseCrafts

www.redbubble.com/people/tortoise-crafts/shop

www.ingramcontent.com/pod-product-compliance
Lightning Source LLC
Chambersburg PA
CBHW041030050726
47599CB00018B/1916